Theology is a Scientific Discipline

Theology is a Scientific Discipline

Dr. Brian Keen

THEOLOGY IS A SCIENTIFIC DISCIPLINE

iUniverse books may be ordered through booksellers or by contacting:

iUniverse
1663 Liberty Drive
Bloomington, IN 47403
www.iuniverse.com
844-349-9409

Because of the dynamic nature of the Internet, any web addresses or links contained in this book may have changed since publication and may no longer be valid. The views expressed in this work are solely those of the author and do not necessarily reflect the views of the publisher, and the publisher hereby disclaims any responsibility for them.

Any people depicted in stock imagery provided by Getty Images are models, and such images are being used for illustrative purposes only. Certain stock imagery © Getty Images.

ISBN: 978-1-6632-7645-2 (sc)
ISBN: 978-1-6632-7646-9 (e)

Print information available on the last page.

iUniverse rev. date: 10/10/2025

Contents

Introduction

The fact that Theology is a Scientific Discipline requires technical terms of reference. As in all true science, it is practical. Technically, this scientific fact was written in my book *Power Living Through Science*, which was based on my doctoral thesis for my Doctor of Theological Studies (DTS) degree, *Summa Cum Laude*.

I am an Orthodox Presbyter ordained on 29th August 1988.

Theology is a scientific discipline. This is an actuality in many parts of the world. The following story is indicative of this reality in the former Soviet Union.

"'The sum total of all that is already known emphasises the unlimited capacity of the human mind, and proves that every natural phenomenon is cognizable,' declared a Russian scientist in 1958. We, Christians, similarly aspire to integral knowledge of being, in the deepest and widest sense. The world of matter does not yet encompass plenitude of being. Without belittling the importance of experimental science, of vital necessity, perhaps, in the struggle for existence, we still cannot overlook its limitations. I once heard the following story of a professor of astronomy who was enthusiastically discoursing in a planetarium on the nebulae and like marvels. Noticing an unpretentious priest who had joined his group of students, the professor asked him:

'What do your Scriptures say about cosmic space and its myriad stars?'

'Instead of giving a direct answer the priest in turn posed a question.

'Tell me, Professor,' he said, 'do you think that science will invent still more powerful telescopes to see even farther into the firmament?'

'Of course progress is possible and science will always be perfecting apparatus for exploring outer space,' replied the astronomer.

'There is hope, then, that one day you will have telescopes that can show all there is in the cosmos, down to the last detail?'

'That would be impossible – the cosmos is infinite,' replied the scientist.

'So there is a limit to science?'

'Yes, in that sense, there is.'

'Well, Professor,' said the priest, 'where your science comes to a full stop, ours begins, and that is what our Scriptures tell of.'"[1]

There is a tremendous amount of theological research available utilizing scientific methodologies. Unfortunately, most of the data is presently not available in English. This book is based upon data available to date. Today there are numerous theological studies based on scientifically verifiable standards.

There was a view that the Orthodox were stopped entirely by the Soviet Union. The book, *Holy Russia Inside The Soviet Union* [2] records the Truth of Orthodox who declare that theology is a scientific discipline.

At https://youtu.be/acVw6N1uM6A Metropolitan Hilarion is awarded for his work of theology as a scientific discipline. Unfortunately, you may not be able to find this material presently. In Russia, his works on theology are recommended for scientific studies in secular tertiary educational institutions. A growing number of theologians

[1] Sophrony, *His Life is Mine*, Oxford, A.R. Mowbray & Co. Ltd., 1977, 57-58
[2] Father, Mitrofan. *Holy Russia Inside the Soviet Union*. Minneapolis, Light and Life Publishing Co., 1989

reject philosophy and have come to recognize the reality that theology is a scientific discipline.

J. Warner Wallace a retired cold case detective used his skills in forensic science to learn the Truth of the Good News. One of his many books is entitled, *Forensic Faith*!

There are numerous theologians of the 20th century such as John Romanides, St. Justin Popovic, and St. Nicholai of Zica who were theologians who utilized scientific methodologies to reach conclusions.

It is my hope that theology will finally be acknowledged as a scientific discipline in the Dominion of Canada.

This should not be surprising to people when it is known that as of 2021, 65.4% of Nobel Prize winners are Christ Followers![3]

Already theology has been accepted for study as a scientific discipline in the Russian Federation with honours being bestowed to Metropolitan Hilarion by President Vladimir Putin.

The 2020 National Award in Literature and Art has been conferred on Metropolitan Hilarion for his contribution to Russian culture and education by President Vladimir Putin.

---

[3] J. Warner Wallace, *Person of Interest*. Grand Rapids, Zondervan Reflective, 2021.

Supposition

This is the Prolegomenon to the position that theology is a scientific discipline. This is based upon scientific methodologies. Theologians must utilize the same laws of methodology as any other scientific research. We utilize the term empirical theologian

The supposition for theology is: there is a god or gods.

A supposition requires a minimal amount of proof. This is true in any scientific research, including theological research. The twofold general classifications within scientific evaluation are: *argumentum a posteriori*, and *argumentum a priori*.[4]

The proofs of the supposition are cosmological, teleological, psychological, and historical.

The cosmological proof is that since the world exists therefore there must be a god or gods. There must be a god or gods to construct the world. A building presupposes a builder. This is a logical conclusion. Every rational person through deductive reasoning upon observing a created structure concludes that there must be someone who has thus created the structure. Consequently, the observation of creation presupposes a creator.

---

[4] For an explanation and tip go to https://www.youtube.com/watch?v=FoHH9_4vKAw

The teleological proof is that the Earth and universe is a great, beautiful, and wondrous work. This observation concludes that there is an intelligent being behind this work. The universe is a work of wondrous purpose and motion, with order and laws, with beauty and grace. The universe is a work that hides within itself a most wise mind and an infinite power that created it. Consider the great readiness and diligence for work displayed by bees and spiders. So great is their love for art that bees create wax so artistically and fragrantly and the spiders weaving their intricate webs with such delicacy, with ethereal threads and such intricate patterns![5] Consider the marvel at the composition and action of water. The nature, the appearance and the taste of water are one and the same. However, its energy has many powers. Water in the grape becomes wine and takes on a new taste. While in the olive it becomes oil and is transformed into bread when mixed with flour.[6]

The psychological proof is that mankind seeks after a god or gods. In the inner recesses of man's nous there is an acknowledgement of His Existence. When one perceives the good and evil in the world, the logical conclusion is that the existence of a god or gods is necessary and inevitable.

The historical proof is that throughout mankind's history there has always been recognition of a god or gods. The great historian Plutarch (born A.D. 46) has stated, "Wherever you go, you may find cities without walls, without schools, without kings, without inhabitants, without currency, without theatres or gymnasia, but an atheist city without the need for prayers and vows, for oracles and sacrifices, for beneficence, you will never see, for such does not exist. It seems to me that one can more easily find a city without ground than one

---

[5] Gregory the Theologian cited by Athanasios S. Frangopoulos, *Our Orthodox Christian Faith*, Athens, The Brotherhood of Theologians, 1988, 45

[6] Cyril of Jerusalem cited by Frangopoulos, 45-46

without religion and belief in God. Such a city cannot exist and should perchance such exist, it cannot endure."[7]

The supposition has proof required to commence research, on the subject of theology as a scientific discipline. From here we will be required to provide more proof. As in all research, there is an assumption.

This means that atheism can only be proved as a negative supposition. Agnosticism is untenable since science requires a supposition that supports the concept of theological research.

Research utilizes the Law of Non-contradiction. Aristotle defined this law as, "the same attribute cannot at the same time belong to the same subject in the same respect."[8]

Research utilizes the Law of Causality that incorporates Aristotle's classification of motion.[9]

Now we must make a determination as to whether there is one or many gods. The proof for One God is the reality of the attributes of the One True God.

The assumption for us to consider in our theological research is God is the Tri-Hypostatical Divinity.[10]

The first step is to consider the attributes of the Tri-Hypostatical Divinity. The attributes of Tri-Hypostatical Divinity consist of Him being omnipresent, omniscient, eternal, immutable, omnipotent, all-wise, holy, righteous, virtuous, and the Truth.

---

[7] *To Kolotes the Epicurean*, 31, cited in ibid, 47. Some might counter that the Soviet Union and the communist bloc had countries that gave precedence to atheism. However, faith groups were never eradicated despite severe persecutions. This experiment failed totally. Refer to Mitrophan's book, *Holy Russia Inside The Soviet Union*, Minneapolis, Light and Life Publishing Co., 1989.

[8] R.C. Sproul, John Gerstner, Arthur Lindsley, *Classical Apologetics*, Grand Rapids, Zondervan Publishing House, 1984, 81.

[9] Ibid, 83.

[10] For a complete explanation of why the term "hypostasis" is relevant, and consequently the "Tri-Hypostatical Divinity" is a more precise term, refer to Symeon the New Theologian, *On The Mystical Life: The Ethical Discourses*, Crestwood, St. Vladimir's Seminary Press, 1997, Volume 3, 123-133.

The omnipresence of the Tri-Hypostatical Divinity indicates that He is not subject to any limitations relating to physical space. The Tri-Hypostatical Divinity sees and oversees everything, whether visible or invisible. There can be no mystery in the One True God, the Tri-Hypostatical Divinity.

As a result of being omnipresent, the consequence, logically, is that the Tri-Hypostatical Divinity must be omniscient. The omniscience of the Tri-Hypostatical Divinity indicates that He is outside of time. Consequently, the Tri-Hypostatical Divinity knows only present. There is no concept of past or future, since everything is present to the Tri-Hypostatical Divinity. His creatures respond to past and future due to their understanding of time. Time is only a form of limited being, changeable being. The omniscience of the Tri-Hypostatical Divinity does not indicate that man's freewill is impinged in any way. The foreknowledge of the Tri-Hypostatical Divinity is not the cause of the occurrence of things, but rather He foreknows that we are to do this or that, thus that which a person is to do, does not have the Tri-Hypostatical Divinity as its cause, but rather a person's own free will.[11]

The eternal nature of the Tri-Hypostatical Divinity indicates that He is ever the same, and as far as time is concerned, has neither beginning nor ending. With reference to the essence of the Tri-Hypostatical Divinity the term means that He never changes but remains continuously the same. This is understood as a natural development of His omniscience. Being omniscient He must be eternal.

The immutable nature of the Tri-Hypostatical Divinity is understood as a direct result of the previous position of His being omniscient and eternal. This un-changeability does not indicate some kind of immovability. Quite the contrary, The Tri-Hypostatical Divinity's Being

---

[11] John Damascene cited by Frangopoulos, 59

is life, filled with [ower and activity. The Tri-Hypostatical Divinity is Himself life, and life is His Being.

The omnipotence of the Tri-Hypostatical Divinity is understood as a direct result of logical sequence. He is Almighty, for how could it be otherwise for the One True God. There is nothing that the Tri-Hypostatical Divinity cannot do, as long as this is extended to everything, which is pleasing to His thought, to His goodness, to His Will.

The attribute of wisdom of the Tri-Hypostatical Divinity is inseparable from His omniscience and is an extension of that attribute. It is the property of the Tri-Hypostatical Divinity to ascertain and determine the most excellent and perfect means whereby His most excellent aims and purposes leads to completion. We see how this is manifest in the reality of the Tri-Hypostatical Divinity, especially in the reality of the Theanthropic Hypostasis.

The attribute of Holiness in the Tri-Hypostatical Divinity indicates that He is pure and free from all moral and ethical imperfection, and is free from and despises sin, wickedness, and depravity. The Tri-Hypostatical Divinity loves only that which is good and just. Consequently, the holiness of the Tri-Hypostatical Divinity is the source of holiness for His creatures.

The attribute of righteousness of the Tri-Hypostatical Divinity is a derivative of His Holiness. He is righteous because He is Holy. Since He hates and despises evil, He must be righteous and does not tolerate any injustice. He judges objectively and without bias. The righteousness of the Tri-Hypostatical Divinity has two aspects: that of lawgiver and that of judge. The laws are all appropriate, such as the Law of Gravity. All laws require judgement. The Law of Gravity works for all creatures upon the Earth.

The attribute of being virtuous of the Tri-Hypostatical Divinity is an extension of His righteousness. As a result, He does not keep His bounties to Himself, but bestows them upon all His creatures. This is indicative of the capacity to love from the Tri-Hypostatical Divinity. The Tri-Hypostatical Divinity has no preference and makes no distinctions.

The attribute of being the Truth is the culmination of all the previously outlined attributes. The Tri-Hypostatical Divinity must be the author of Truth. The Tri-Hypostatical Divinity always possesses Truth, or rather, He is Truth, and loves Truth, and speaks Truth to all creation. Theology declares that Truth is not a concept but a Hypostasis. We shall see later, when we look at the reality of the Tri-Hypostatical Divinity what the significance to this actuality is.

We can now conclude that there can be only One True God, the Tri-Hypostatical Divinity. From this vantage point, we can conclude that some theological positions are in error. For instance, polytheism is wrong when assessed in light of research utilizing scientific methodologies as we shall see in the following paragraphs. This brings us to the position that the following faith groups are the only ones that are viable: Christianity, Orthodox, Islam, and Judaism. We must proceed to see if the one True God is the Tri-Hypostatical Divinity.

One of the areas of dispute among the proponents of the One True God is with reference to whether He has a name. The problem with this is that a name is usual when one addresses another like being. God has no equal who can address Him. The only way that this can be plausible is for God to manifest Himself in a form that allows equal access to mankind. Let us first consider the potential names presented by the various faith groups who understand the One True God, but do not necessarily subscribe to the position of the Tri-Hypostatical Divinity.

To a theologian who is a proponent of Islam, God's name is "Allah." Unfortunately, Allah is unknown outside of Islamic theological works.

Theologians who are proponents of Judaism accept a number of personal names. Adonai is the unique, personal name of God and the name most frequently used in *The Torah*. The original pronunciation was most likely "Yahveh", but since Jewish tradition permitted the name to be voiced only by the High Priest it became customary, after the destruction of the Second Temple, to substitute the word Adonai (meaning "my Lord").[12]

The other popular name for God is Elohim. However, Elohim is the generic term for divinity most frequently found in the Bible. It is used as a plural noun for gods of other nations and as a singular noun when applied to Israel's God.[13]

Some Christian theologians assert that Jehovah or Yahveh is God's name. Unfortunately, a Christian writer of the sixteenth century was unaware of the substitution made by the Masoretes in *The Torah*. They placed the vowels from the word "Adonai" and put them with Yahveh to remind the reader not to read "Yahveh" but "Adonai." As a result, the word "Jehovah" erroneously entered many Christian Bible translations.[14]

Many theologians support the position that the most reasonable name for God is Jesus. This has viability, especially when utilizing the concept of the Theanthropic Nature of Jesus of Nazareth. The name Jesus means "Saviour"[15] which is attributed to the Tri-Hypostatical Divinity.

There are other names, which will be addressed further under Christology.

---

[12] W. Gunther Plaut, ed., *The Torah: A Modern Commentary*, New York, Union of American Hebrew Congregations, 1981, 31.
[13] Ibid.
[14] Ibid.
[15] Theophylact of Ochrid and Bulgaria, *The Explanation of The Holy Gospel According to St. Matthew*, House Springs, Chrysostom Press, 1993, 13.

These faith groups should also be assessed through theological research. We need to assess the validity of our proposed conclusion.

Now, we will evaluate the supposition that the One True God is the Tri-Hypostatical Divinity. This indicates that God has One Essence, yet there are three Hypostases. The Hypostases have hypostatic attributes.

The principal reason for acceptance of the Tri-Hypostatical Divinity is the Law of Love. In order for the One True God to be the author of the Law of Love, He must be able to express this reality.

The concept of the Tri-Hypostatical Divinity indicates the fullness of the mystical inward life in the One True God, for He is Love. This theological supposition proves correct, thus leading us to the conclusion that the Tri-Hypostatical Divinity is the One True God. Let us further evaluate these proofs.

The reason for the number three in the Tri-Hypostatical Divinity is based upon the concept that: the element of conjoint action as two experiences, there must be a third who serves as object.[16] There is no reason for more than three, yet there could not be less. On this ground of fact within a triad of Hypostases every demand which reciprocity might present is satisfied.

The Tri-Hypostatical Divinity is understood as: God the Father, God the Son, and God the Holy Spirit.

The Symbol of Faith, also known as the Creed, clearly and concisely delineates the roles of each Hypostasis in the Tri-Hypostatical Divinity. The Symbol of Faith states:

I.   I believe in one God, Father Almighty, Maker of heaven and earth and of all things visible and invisible.

II.   And in one Lord Jesus Christ, the Son of God, the Only-begotten, begotten of the Father before all worlds. Light of

---

[16] As in triangulation

8

Light, very God of very God: begotten, not made, of one essence with the Father, through whom all things are made.

III. Who for us men and for our salvation came down from heaven, and became incarnate of the Holy Spirit and the Virgin Mary, and became a man.

IV. And was crucified for us under Pontius Pilate, and suffered, and was buried.

V. And rose again on the third day according to the Scriptures.

VI. And ascended into heaven, and sitteth at the right hand of the Father.

VII. And shall come again with glory to judge the living and the dead, and whose Kingdom shall have no end.

VIII. And in the Holy Spirit, the Lord, the Giver of Life, who proceedeth from the Father, who with the Father and the Son is worshiped and glorified, and who spake through the prophets.

IX. In one, holy, catholic, and apostolic Church.

X. I acknowledge one baptism, for the remission of sins.

XI. I look for the Resurrection of the dead.

XII. And life in the world to come. Amen.[17]

The Symbol of Faith was enumerated at the first two Ecumenical Councils, which were convened in Nicaea (A.D. 325) and Constantinople (A.D. 381). The Symbol of Faith has been continuously ratified, by the entire Ecclesia and at subsequent Ecumenical Councils (i.e., there have been a total of seven Ecumenical Councils).

God the Father is understood to be Unbegotten.

Unlike the other Hypostases, there is not much study of God the

---

[17] Nicodemus and Agapius,(ed.) *The Rudder*, West Brookfield, The Orthodox Christian Educational Society, 1983, vii

Father that is as extensive in theological research. In the case of God the Son, theologians have developed Christology. This is due, in part, to our slavery to time and space. God the Father is less present in time and space to us than the other two Hypostases. Augustine of Hippo clearly explains the dichotomy for us:

"For how could countless ages pass by if you had not made them, since you are the source and creator of all ages? What times could those be which were not made by you? And how could ages pass if they did not exist? Therefore, since you are the creator of all times, if any time existed before you made heaven and earth, why is it said that you refrained from working? For you made that same time, and times could not pass by before you made them. But if before heaven and earth there was no time, why do they ask what you were then doing? For there was no 'then' when time was not."[18]

It is understood that God the Son is pre-eternally Begotten. This is presented in the Hypostasis, known in history as Jesus of Nazareth. There is sufficient proof of His Reality, and His claim of being Incarnate of God the Father. Jesus of Nazareth establishes His Ecclesia consecrating twelve people to the Episcopate, with the Apostolic Office. When the 12 were trained thy trained others to make 70 Apostles. Jesus designates his half-brother, James, to be the first to be consecrated to the Episcopate in the Mother Ecclesia of Jerusalem. This is an historical fact.

It is understood that God the Holy Spirit proceeds from the Father. The Holy Spirit is responsible for the Ecclesia. Consequently, the Ecclesia is an Eternal Organism. All other Ecclesia designations proceed from the Mother Ecclesia of Jerusalem. This is a reality based upon historical data.

---

[18] Augustine of Hippo, *Confessions*, London, The Folio Society, 1993, .217

How can we confirm this position with so many conflicting theological positions concerning the conclusion of the Tri-Hypostatical Divinity? We will look at His Manifestations concerning the Mother Ecclesia of Jerusalem, and later we will look at Miraculous Occurrences manifest by the Tri-Hypostatical Divinity.

Bibliology

Empirical research confirms that the Tri-Hypostatical Divinity communicates to mankind through various written media. The primary methodology of this communication is known as *The Holy Bible*.

This brings us to the reality of biblical theology. Although biblical theology has deficiencies, the claim that *The Holy Bible* is the Word of God has credence since only this claimant has the scientific proof of the Tri-Hypostatical Divinity.

It should be remembered that *The Holy Bible* is not a theological treatise. *The Holy Bible* claims to be written by The Tri-Hypostatical Divinity for all of mankind. This is Revelation from the Tri-Hypostatical Divinity to mankind. This does not mean that this is the only Written Word. The Tri-Hypostatical Divinity has made His Presence known so that He may be evaluated through scientific research. The first known written Revelation was given to Enoch, the first scientist and the inventor of writing.

The Holy Bible is unique in that there are human authors who claim that they were speaking on behalf of the Tri-Hypostatical Divinity. This is understood through the concept of dual authorship through the theanthropic methodology. In evaluating the entire spectrum of whether inerrancy is a viable theological conclusion, it is quite pertinent to read the book, *Inerrancy*.[19] Let us evaluate biblical inerrancy.

The book, *Inerrancy*[20] attempts to prove that *The Holy Bible* is the Inerrant Word of the Tri-Hypostatical Divinity. This excellent book misses one key component, however. There is a faulty supposition that Scripture produces the Ecclesia. No one ever explains how this is possible. The Ecclesia comes to the Earth A.D. 33.

Let us first assess the supposition that *The Holy Bible* produced the Ecclesia. This supposition was presented because of the Reformation. This is understandable in light of the fact that, during this era, the Roman Patriarchate defined Scripture. Books of Scripture were known, so there was a natural concern about ascertaining if the Roman Patriarchate constituted the Ecclesia. The Reformation was an attempt to change the perceived inadequacies of the Roman Patriarchate. With the supposition that Scripture produced the Ecclesia there was confirmation that the Roman Patriarchate held deficiencies as the Ecclesia. Faith became an important aspect in determining the correct Ecclesia. Faith was found in the correct interpretation of Scripture. The problem with this supposition is that the Reformation found that Scripture had inadequacies when attempting to understand the structure and systems of the Ecclesia. The end result was Protestantism, which led to numerous claimants to being the Ecclesia, along with numerous modes of baptism, structures, and systems. The conclusion is that the supposition contains serious errors. The proliferation of claimants to the Ecclesia is truly indicative of this error. Consequently, the conclusion is that the supposition fails. *The Holy Bible* does not produce the Ecclesia.

'The Roman Patriarchate has a differing view not evaluated in

---

[19] Norman L. Geisler, ed., *Inerrancy*, Grand Rapids, Zondervan Publishing House, 1980.
[20] Dr. Norman Geisler is an exceptional theologian who served as President of the Evangelical Theological Society (ETS) in 1998. In full disclosure, the author is an Associate Member of ETS.

Inerrancy. Let us consider this supposition presented by the Roman Patriarchate in the claim to being the Ecclesia. This supposition is that the Ecclesia produces Scripture. The difference between this supposition and the one presented below is based upon the application. Sadly, this is an aspect that has not been evaluated by many theologians doing research. The Roman Patriarchate supports the concept that the Ecclesia is under the leadership of His Holiness, the Pope of Rome, who is considered the Head of the Ecclesia. It is the Patriarchate of Rome that ascertains which Books constitute Scripture. There is a major problem with this position. How can any individual man be the Head of the Ecclesia? We have seen above that the intent of the Reformation was originally to produce a development within the Patriarchate to grant recognition of faith. Popes of Rome had failed to recognize the necessity of faith, which Scripture describes as the first step in the journey in the Ecclesia.[21] The claims of the Patriarchate are evaluated thoroughly in the book *The Rush to Embrace*.[22] The contradictions of the Patriarchate of Rome lead to the conclusion that this supposition suffers from severe problems. The conclusion is that the Ecclesia cannot produce Scripture, when one considers His Holiness, the Pope is assumed to be the Head of the Ecclesia as opposed to the Theanthropos Who is in Truth is the only Head of the Ecclesia.[23]

Let us now consider the supposition that: the Ecclesia produces Scripture. This is thoroughly assessed but considers the concept that the Ecclesia can only have One Eternal Head, the Theanthropos. No human can adequately Head the Ecclesia. While all claimants to the Ecclesia have earthly leaders only one claimant has no earthly leader.

---

[21] Refer to *Galatians* 2:16
[22] Alexey Young, *The Rush to Embrace*, Richfield Springs, Nikodemos Orthodox Publication Society, 1996
[23] Justin Popovich, Orthodox *Faith and Life in Christ,* Belmont, The Institute for Byzantine and Modern Greek Studies, 1994, 104

'The only claimant of the Ecclesia that has no earthly leader is described as Orthodox. She is also described as the One, Holy, Catholic, and Apostolic Ecclesia as the Symbol of Faith declares. She is also declared as Orthodox in the Synodikon which states, "As the prophets beheld, as the Apostles have taught, as the Church has received, as the Teachers have dogmatized, as the Universe has agreed, as Grace has shown forth; as Truth has revealed, as falsehood has been dissolved, as Wisdom has presented, as Christ awarded, let Us declare, let Us assert, let Us preach in like manner Christ our true God, and honor His Saints in words, in writings, in thoughts, in deeds, in churches, in Holy Icons – worshiping Him as God and Lord and honoring Them as His true servants and accordingly offering them veneration. This is the Faith of the Apostles; this is the Faith which has established the Universe."[24]

The history that encompasses *The Holy Bible* entails a number of centuries. The initial Scripture describes the Creation, while the latter describes the re-Creation. Not all Scripture is related to any aspects of the Ecclesia. Most of the Old Testament has importance in describing the Law of the Tri-Hypostatical Divinity prior to the entering of the Ecclesia into time. This has relevance to mankind but is not pertinent to Soteriology since the Ecclesia is declaring the Good News Message based upon Love rather than Law.

The Books of *The Holy Bible* commenced A.D. 37, yet confirmation is not attested to until the Council of Laodicea until 363.[25] How does the Ecclesia exist while Scripture is being written? The tremendous growth of the Ecclesia indicates that the Hypostasis known as the Holy Spirit directs Her and the Theanthropos continues as Her only Head. Scripture is written and confirmed by and through the Ecclesia. An

[24] Mihajlo Doder, *Vespers For The Sunday of Orthodoxy*, Mississauga, All Serbian Saints Serbian Orthodox Church, 2003.
[25] J. Warner Wallace, Cold-Case Christianity, Updated & Extended Edition, Colorada Springs, David C. Cook, 2023, 298-299.

example of this is *the Book of Revelation*, which is a Message from the Theanthropos to John the Theologian.[26] John the Theologian sends this message to the seven Ecclesiastical Communities in the Roman Province of Asia.[27] This clearly shows how communications function within the Ecclesia. *The Book of Revelation* does not give instructions on how the Ecclesiastical communications should take place. The Ecclesia acknowledges that John the Theologian holds the Episcopate as Metropolitan responsible for the Province of Asia, since his See is Ephesus. The fact that this is acknowledged by the Ecclesia destroys any claimants to Ecclesiastical recognition who do not recognize this structure.

The scientific fact is that the Ecclesia as an Eternal Organism produces Scripture. *The Holy Bible* commences with the *Book of Genesis* and ends with the *Book of Revelation*. The Head of the Ecclesia, the Theanthropos, is called the Word,[28] while *The Holy Bible* is also called the Word (of God). This is not a coincidence, but a reality. The Theanthropos is the Word of the Tri-Hypostatical Divinity as the declarer of communication with mankind. He proclaims verbally (*Genesis* 1) as well as in writing (*Revelation* 1). The Theanthropos is quoted in *Inerrancy* as recognizing the Truth of Scripture, when He was known as Jesus of Nazareth.

Let us evaluate the supposition that: the Ecclesia produces Scripture. The Ecclesia is an Eternal Organism established by the Tri-Hypostatical Divinity. The Ecclesia comes into time through those whom the Theanthropos has ordained to the Episcopate. The Coming of the Ecclesia into time is the Day of Pentecost A.D. 33 when the Faithful were filled with the one Hypostasis known as the Holy Spirit (*Acts* 2).

---

[26] Refer to Revelation 1: 1
[27] Refer to Revelation 1:4
[28] Refer to John 1:1

The Ecclesia continues throughout time without change or alteration to the principal aspects of Her existence.

Communications from the Tri-Hypostatical Divinity to mankind prior to the Ecclesia coming into time is acknowledged through Apostolic Canon and continues to have ratification. Mankind knows these communications as the Old Testament. The Ecclesia accepts the Septuagint as the appropriate Old Testament document. Translations should be based upon this document, keeping in mind the Conscience of the Ecclesia. The Conscience of the Ecclesia is the complete discernment of the totality of the Faithful. The Ecclesia must make judgements based upon the entire acceptance of the Faithful.

The Ecclesia now receives special communications from the Tri-Hypostatical Divinity that is known to mankind as the New Testament. The Ecclesia assesses the appropriate worthiness of all writings to ascertain the relevant Truth. Although the Apostolic Canon 85 makes a declaration of the Books of the *Holy Bible* there is an acknowledgement of the conscience of the Ecclesia. There has never been a declaration of the Books from any Ecumenical Council. The conscience of the Ecclesia is the general recognition of Truth that requires one hundred per cent acknowledgment. The Head of the Ecclesia is the Truth;[29] consequently the Ecclesia follows the decisions of Her Head.

The Ecclesia continues to ratify the *Books* of *The Holy Bible*. Throughout recorded history the Ecclesia has assessed *Books* for value, and changes the inner contents, such as the removal of the two Epistles of *Clement*. Throughout the designation of *The Holy Bible* from the Ecclesia the first Book has been *Genesis* while the last *Book* has been the *Revelation*. This is the Will of the Tri-Hypostatical Divinity as given to the Ecclesia. The internal Books of *The Holy Bible* are based upon the need of the Faithful in the declaration of the Good News Message

---

[29] Refer to John 14:6

to the world and universe. It is neither within the purview of the understanding nor the interpretation of the individual, whether Faithful or not, to understand Scripture.[30] Consequently the understanding must be validated by the entire Ecclesia. There is no other interpretation that can bear this scrutiny.

The Ecclesia proves definitively that *The Holy Bible* is positively the Inerrant Word of the Tri-Hypostatical Divinity. Since the Ecclesia is an Eternal Organism She has Her Head, Truth. She cannot produce lies, since She is committed to Truth. The Tri-Hypostatical Divinity governs the Ecclesia. Decisions of the Ecclesia are proposed through the phrase, "it seemed good to the Holy Spirit, and to us,"[31] which then is ratified by the entire Ecclesia. "Worthy" is declared by all of the Faithful for major decisions, including the ordination to the Mystery of Holy Orders during the Divine Liturgy.[32]

`The Theanthropos is the Head of the Ecclesia and He acknowledges the reality of Scripture. He acknowledges this in *The Holy Bible*, as clearly expressed in *Inerrancy*. Since He is the Theanthropos He is well aware of the reality of Scripture. He is one Hypostasis of the Tri-Hypostatical Divinity and He has always been the Head of the Ecclesia. It is the Theanthropos who brings the Ecclesia to Earth, since He teaches, trains, preaches, and organizes the initial disciples to form the Ecclesia awaiting the formal re-Creation of the Ecclesia on the Day of Pentecost A.D. 33. The Theanthropos ordained the Episcopates who acted in the capacity of Apostles,[33] and it was these twelve that constituted the first of Episcopate as leaders in the Ecclesia.

The Theanthropos as Head of the Ecclesia taught the first Divine

---

[30] Refer to 2 Peter 1: 20- 21

[31] Acts 15:28

[32] Philip, *Service Book*, Englewood Hills, Antiochian Orthodox Christian Archdiocese of North America, 1984. Ordination: to diaconate 233, to Presbyter 236, to Protopresbyter (Dean) 237, to Archimandrite 238.

[33] Refer to Mark 3:14

Liturgy to James the first of Episcopate of the Mother Ecclesiastical Community of Jerusalem. The Gospel Book is honoured during the Little Entrance of the Divine Liturgy. The Ecclesia has the perspective of evaluating Scripture. This is due to reality that She exists in time. This is referred to as the Ecclesia Militant. She also has the reality of being eternal, referred to as the Ecclesia Triumphant. The Ecclesia is One despite the two aspects of Her existence. The Theanthropos clarifies that Scripture is meant for the One Ecclesia.[34]

The Theanthropos continues as Head of the Ecclesia, issuing directives. *The Gospel Book* is honoured during the Little Entrance of the Divine Liturgy. *The Gospel Book* is usually covered in gold or other magnificent material. *The Gospel Book* is presented over his left shoulder of one who is called to Holy Orders, with precedence given to one called to the diaconate, during the procession of lights. The Faithful bow and do obeisance as the one bearing *the Gospel Book* enters through the Prothesis (North door of the Iconostasis) through the main portion of the Temple with a stop in front of the Royal Doors. The person carrying *the Gospel Book* aloft acclaims "Wisdom! Let us attend!"[35] to all of the Faithful. The Sign of the Cross is made with *the Gospel Book*. The procession then enters the Royal Doors, with all the Faithful bowing and performing obeisance. When the Good News Message is proclaimed the response of the Faithful is as if the Theanthropos is personally there. The proclamation is done in front of the icon of the Theanthropos, or from the Ambo. All the Faithful stand and perform the appropriate obeisance as the Good News Message is chanted. This commences with the acclamation of the cantors declaring, with the Ethereal Beings, "Alleluia! Alleluia! Alleluia!"[36] The acclamation after

---

[34] Refer to Matthew 5:17-19

[35] +Jonah, *Service Books of the Orthodox Church*, Second Edition, St. Tikhon's Seminary Press, South Canaan, Pennsylvania, 2010, 41

[36] Ibid, 45

the chanting of the Holy Gospel is "Glory to Thee, O Lord, glory to Thee."[37] This has great significance since the original text of the Divine Liturgy is given by the Theanthropos, yet there are changes by Basil the Great and John Chrysostom.

`Inerrancy is scientifically provable when understanding the Ecclesia.

What are the benefits of the Ecclesia producing the inerrant Scripture, known as *The Holy Bible*?

The first aspect is the reliability of the texts when understood through the Conscience of the Ecclesia. There is never any doubt as to the historical data contained since the Ecclesia has existed prior to time. Her observation of history is impeccable. Should there appear to be a conflict, it requires more data from human research.

The theologians are free to research various concepts without worrying about restrictions to Scriptural language. *The Holy Bible* is a written communication from the Tri-Hypostatical Divinity to all mankind regardless of educational background. It is not a theological treatise designed for those holding a specific degree in theology, such as the Evangelical Theological Society requiring a Masters degree in theology. The terms "Tri-Hypostatical Divinity" and "Theanthropos" are precise theological definitions.

The structure of the Ecclesia clarifies why Scripture is written the way that it is presented to mankind. For instance, theologians and people not accepting this basic conclusion are perplexed as to whom the Theanthropos is communicating with in *the Book of Revelation*. The recipient is named, as John yet there seems to be confusion about his position. Since Scripture only speaks of "bishops", the divisions of those holding the Episcopate create problems for some theologians, never mind the Faithful. The reality is that those holding the Episcopate are Apostle (one who travels, introducing the Ecclesia in an area), Metropolitan

---

[37] Ibid

(one who serves in a capital who presides at Councils), and Bishop (one who presides in an Ecclesiastical Community). Understanding this helps us to confirm that John the Theologian was the recipient of the *Revelation*. He accepts the communication in his capacity as Metropolitan of Ephesus. John the Theologian was an Apostle, yet since he settled in Ephesus with the Theotokos, his responsibility was within the scope of Metropolitan. Many theologians do not understand this aspect of these roles. All the above comes from *The Rudder*, Apostolic Canons. None of the Apostolic Canons are appropriate for Scripture.

There is great confusion about the Mysteries of the Ecclesia, and the mode of specific ones such as the Mystery of Baptism. Many claimants to being the Ecclesia have varying views of the Mystery of Baptism, some claiming that this is not even necessary. The Ecclesia declares the reality of Mysteries and the proper mode of baptism. Aside from this declaration there is the research of the correct mode of baptism performed by modern Judaism that follows the methodology instituted by the Levitical Priesthood. In both cases the correct system of baptism is related to unwritten Tradition. In the case of the Ecclesia, this is referred to as Oral Sacred Tradition.

Through disseminating Oral Sacred Tradition Basil the Great confirms this reality of the correct mode of baptism.[38]

The Ecclesia clarifies when the Faithful are eligible for ordination and what ranks there are in the Mystery of Holy Orders. *The Holy Bible* speaks of specific ranks (e.g., bishop), while alluding to others (e.g., the diaconate, in *Acts* 6). However, there are no specifics provided, so that some claimants to the Ecclesia have bishops covering many communities, while others have no bishops at all. Consequently, *The Holy Bible* is inadequate to present the specific requirements and ranks of those called to Holy Orders in the Ecclesia. The primary source in the

---

[38] St. Basil the Great, *On The Holy Spirit*, Crestwood, St. Vladimir's Seminary Press, 1980, 99.

Ecclesia for guidelines of those called to Holy Orders is *The Rudder*.[39] This also clarifies the reality that Scripture is written communications to mankind. Otherwise, the various claimants of being the Ecclesia would be of one opinion about whom and when ordinations are appropriate. This is a proof of the Ecclesia producing Scripture.

The Mystery of Matrimony is an extremely important aspect of the Ecclesia. *The Holy Bible* does not indicate any guidelines for the Faithful. A joke indicates the methodologies of matrimony according to Scripture. These are:

1. Find an attractive prisoner of war, bring her home shave her head, trim her nails, and give her new clothes. Then she's yours. (Deuteronomy 21:11-13)

2. Find a prostitute and marry her. (Hosea 1:1-3)

3. Find a man with seven daughters and impress him by watering his flock. (Exodus 2:16-21)

4. Purchase a piece of property and get a woman as part of the deal. (Ruth 4:5-10)

5. Go to a party and hide. When the women come out to dance, grab one and carry her off to be your wife. (Judges 21:19-25)

6. Have God create a wife for you while you sleep. Note: this will cost you. (Genesis 2:19-24)

7. Agree to work seven years in exchange for a woman's hand in marriage. Get tricked into marrying the wrong woman. Then work another seven years for the woman you wanted to marry in the first place. That's right. Fourteen years of toil for a wife. (Genesis 29:15-30)

---

[39] Almost the entire eighty-five (85) Canons of the Holy and Renowned Apostles are specific guidelines for those are under Holy Orders, 1-154. Refer to Nicodemus.

8. Cut 200 foreskins for your future father-in-law's enemies and get his daughter for a wife. (1 Samuel 18:27)

9. Become the emperor of a huge nation and hold a beauty contest. (Esther 2:3-4)

10. When you see someone, you like, go home and tell your parents, "I have seen a woman; now get her for me." If your parents question your decision, simply say, "Get her for me. She's the one for me." (Judges 14:1-3)

11. Kill a husband and take his wife. (2 Samuel 11)

12. Wait for your brother to die. Take his widow. (Deuteronomy, Leviticus, and Ruth)

13. Marry a number of women. (1 Kings 11:1-3)

14. Not to marry at all. (1 Corinthians 7:32-35)

How many claimants to the Ecclesia would be favourably disposed to any of the fourteen? The Ecclesia has specific guidelines for the Mystery of Matrimony in *The Rudder*.[40]

The Ecclesia produces Scripture. The Theanthropos is the Head of the Ecclesia and He acknowledges the reality of Scripture. He is recorded as supporting Scripture. The book *Inerrancy* does an excellent appraisal of this fact. The research is beyond reproach. This is a scientific conclusion available to theologians.

This is an aspect of the Ecclesia, since She is the recipient and the holder of *The Holy Bible.* Further proofs relating to the Ecclesia are found under theological research relating to Ecclesiology in Chapter 8.

Canon 85 of the Holy and Renowned Apostles enumerates the Books of *The Holy Bible.* The Books in the Old Testament are: Genesis, Exodus, Leviticus, Numbers, Deuteronomy, Joshua, Judges, Ruth, 1st

---

[40] There is a specific section entitled "Concise and Accurate Instructions Concerning Marriages" 977-999. Refer to Nicodemus.

Kings, 2ⁿᵈ Kings, 3ʳᵈ Kings, 4ᵗʰ Kings, 1ˢᵗ Chronicles, 2ⁿᵈ Chronicles, 1ˢᵗ Esdras, 2ⁿᵈ Esdras, Nehemiah, Tobit, Judith, Esther, 1ˢᵗ Maccabees, 2ⁿᵈ Maccabees, 3ʳᵈ Maccabees, Psalms, Job, Proverbs of Solomon, Ecclesiastes, Song of Songs, Wisdom of Solomon, Wisdom of Sirach, Hosea, Amos, Micah, Joel, Obadiah, Jonah, Nahum, Habakkuk, Zephaniah, Haggai, Zechariah, Malachi, Isaiah, Jeremiah, Baruch, Lamentations of Jeremiah, Epistle of Jeremiah, Ezekiel, and Daniel. These books are translated from the Septuagint version, and continue to be utilized by the Ecclesia, none having been repudiated by the Ecclesia.

`The Books of the New Testament, approved in Canon 85 of the Holy and Renowned Apostles are enumerated as: Matthew, Mark, Luke, John, Acts of the Apostles, 14 Epistles of Paul (i.e., Romans, 1ˢᵗ Corinthians, 2ⁿᵈ Corinthians, Galatians, Ephesians, Philippians, Colossians, 1ˢᵗ Thessalonians, 2ⁿᵈ Thessalonians, 1ˢᵗ Timothy, 2ⁿᵈ Timothy, Titus, Philemon, and Hebrews), 2 Epistles of Peter (i.e., 1ˢᵗ and 2ⁿᵈ Peter), 3 Epistles of John (i.e., 1ˢᵗ, 2ⁿᵈ, 3ʳᵈ John), one Epistle of James, one Epistle of Jude, 2 Epistles of Clement (i.e., 1ˢᵗ and 2ⁿᵈ Clement), and the Injunctions. The Ecclesia later rejected the following Books: all the Epistles and Injunctions from Clement. The Ecclesia later accepted the Book of Revelation as Scripture.[41]

The Holy Bible is the Word of God since it is affirmed by the Theanthropos as Head of the Ecclesia and is confirmed by God the Holy Spirit through the Ecclesia. The affirmation by God the Holy Spirit through the Ecclesia is confirmed by the Jerusalem Council and subsequent Councils with the phraseology of "For it seemed good to the Holy Spirit and to us…" [42]

The Holy Bible is a key element in further understanding of the Tri-Hypostatical Divinity, which confirms all His attributes. Christians,

---

[41] Nicodemus, 145-146.
[42] Acts 15:28

Orthodox, and Disciples in agreement with the concept of the New Covenant from the Tri-Hypostatical Divinity. We shall confine our research to the New Covenant, since there is agreement only to this point.

The Holy Bible confirms the attribute of omnipresence for it states, "there is no creature hidden from His sight, but all things *are* naked and open to the eyes of Him to whom we *must give* account."[43]

The attribute of omniscience is confirmed, "Jesus, knowing their thoughts, said, 'Why do you think evil in your hearts?'"[44]

The attribute of eternal existence is confirmed, "John, to the seven churches which are in Asia: Grace to you and peace from Him who is and who was and who is to come, and from the seven Spirits who are before His throne."[45]

The attribute of immutability is confirmed, "Every good gift and every perfect gift is from above, and comes down from the Father of lights, with whom there is no variation or shadow of turning."[46]

The attribute of omnipotence is confirmed, "For with God nothing will be impossible."[47]

The attribute of being the source of wisdom is confirmed, "Now to the King eternal, immortal, invisible, to God who alone is wise, *be* honor and glory forever and ever. Amen."[48]

The attribute of being holy is confirmed, "but as He who called you *is* holy, you also be holy in all *your* conduct, because it is written, *'Be holy, for I am holy.'*"[49]

The attribute of righteousness is confirmed, "And I heard another

---

[43] Hebrews 4:13
[44] Matthew 9:4
[45] *Revelation* 1:4
[46] James 1:17
[47] Luke 1:37
[48] 1 Timothy 1:17
[49] 1 Peter 1:15, 16

from the altar saying, 'Even so, Lord God Almighty, true and righteous *are* Your judgments.'"[50]

The attribute of virtuous existence is confirmed, "that you may be sons of your Father in heaven; for He makes His sun rise on the evil and on the good, and sends rain on the just and on the unjust."[51]

The attribute of Truth is confirmed, "Jesus said to him, 'I am the way, the truth, and the life. No one comes to the Father except through Me.'"[52]

Another proof is that every major faith group acknowledges the validity of *The Holy Bible*. Hinduism, Judaism (who accept only the portion described as *The Torah*), Orthodox, Islam, and Christianity all regard this as Scripture. This is amazing recognition of being God's Word to all of mankind.

Some might question the reality of Miraculous Occurrences in *The Holy Bible*. Let us consider what Galileo teaches: that all bodies, irrespective of their specific weight, fall to earth with the same speed and acceleration. However, it is a generally known fact that a bit of fluff falls to the ground much more slowly than an iron weight, in contradiction to this Law. Wood does not fall when it is in water. This Law is not broken by the reality of an airplane flying rather than falling. As in the Law presented by Galileo, as for all Laws of Nature, there is within it a silent reservation: "subject to various conditions," or "if all outside influences are held constant." [53]

Consequently, if the Theanthropos is said to walk on water as on dry land, then this does not contradict the Law of Gravity anymore than the examples cited above. In the latter instances, the Law of Gravity is not broken, but is overcome by the power of the water and the power

---

[50] Revelation 16:7
[51] Matthew 5:45
[52] John 14:6
[53] Seraphim Slobodskoy, *The Law of God*, Jordanville, Holy Trinity Monastery, 1996, 442.

of the airplane's engine. The Tri-Hypostatical Divinity has the Power to overcome the Law of Gravity.

There must be further research to confirm the supposition that there is a god or gods.

The Holy Bible has viability as a document in determining ethical standards.

We shall present basic proofs relating to: Christology, Angelology, Anthropology, Hamartiology, Soteriology, Ecclesiology, Eschatology, and Pneumatology.

It is evident that the Truth conveys His Message to mankind through His Word, known as *The Holy Bible*. Research proves that this is an inerrant communication, useful for empirical theologians to understand the Creator of the Universe. There is no detriment to anyone understanding what is communicated by the Truth. There may be misunderstanding, yet the best way to evaluate any source is to read the communication, especially when the Source is the Truth.

New Data:

Since 2010 there has been further conformation relating to bibliological research.

In archeology, there have been major breakthroughs that are somewhat controversial in that scientific discipline. This is where theology comes in, as a scientific discipline. It is important to have multidisciplinary research to ascertain the correct conclusions. In the "Patterns of Evidence" series on the Exodus DVD, to theologians the dates should not be decided before finding the evidence. The evidence presented for the reality of Joseph and the Exodus must be evaluated as recommended by the archaeologist David Rohl, rather than picking a date to refute the theological conclusion in bibliology. Theologians as well as interested people should see this DVD.

The Canadian Orthodox has accepted *The Orthodox Study Bible* as the Authorized Bible for Orthodox in the Dominion of Canada.

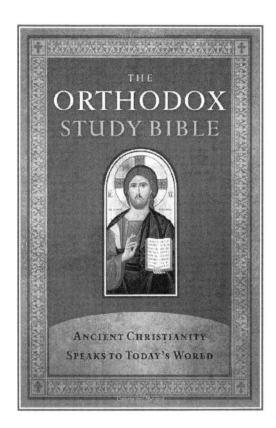

Christology

The next progression is whether the Tri-Hypostatical Divinity has come to the Earth as a human being. The Theanthropos is the most exacting title of Yeshua, who is known generally as Jesus of Nazareth. The scientific evaluation is called Christology.

We now present historical and corroborating proofs relating to Christology.

We will look at various aspects of the life of Jesus of Nazareth and see if this has been duplicated and recorded by historians and/or researchers.

Research confirms that Jesus of Nazareth is the Theanthropos. "The communicatio idiomatum of the one nature to the other is of the divine nature to the human, and of the human to the divine. What does this mean? It means that the idiomata of the one nature of the Theanthropos are ascribed to the other nature and vice versa. Idiomata of the divine nature are divine all-wisdom, and all-omniscience, all-powerfulness, omnipresence, goodness and mercy, holiness and sinlessness – though sinlessness is a property of His human nature as well. His human attributes are hunger, thirst, fatigue, sleep, suffering, and death."[54]

---

[54] Frangopoulos, 145-146

An historical confirmation of the Transfiguration occurred in the nineteenth century. Nicholas Alexandrovich Motovilo had the following encounter with Seraphim of Sarov. They were discussing the Transfiguration of the Theanthropos on Mount Tabor. As the discussion ensued, Seraphim's face was similar to the centre of the sun, in the most dazzling brilliance of its noontime rays, as he was speaking. Nicholas could see the movement of his lips and the changing expression of Seraphim's eyes, hear his voice, and feel him holding his shoulders. Due to the blinding light, spreading around for several metres, which was illuminating with its brilliant sheen both the bank of snow covering the glade and the snowflakes that fell on both of them.[55]

The reality of the Theanthropos can be confirmed through the authenticity of the Holy Cross. It is an historical fact that the Roman Empress, Helen, and Macarius the Episcopate of the Ecclesiastical Community of Jerusalem found the Holy Cross. Initially three crosses were found buried by researchers. It was determined that should one have significance to the cross, there should be something to confirm this reality. On the advice of Macarius, the crosses were brought one at a time to a very sick woman. Nothing happened after the first two crosses were brought, but when the third cross was brought, she immediately became well. Through this methodology it was determined that this may be the Holy Cross, through which the Theanthropos worked Miraculous Occurrences.[56]

Further research indicates that the properties of the Holy Cross are unique. The Holy Cross sinks in water (as opposed to most wood which would float) and continues to grow. This is confirmed by Efstathios Kontoravdis, who had a small portion of the Holy Cross in his possession. He is now reposed.

---

[55] Constantine Cavarnos, and Mary-Barbara Zeldin, *St. Seraphim of Sarov*, Belmont, Institute for Byzantine and Modern Greek Studies, 1980, 110-14.
[56] Slobodskoy, 400.

Among the cited Miraculous Occurrences, the most spectacular is the account of the raising of Lazarus. Lazarus became Episcopate of Kition in Cyprus.

There are numerous confirmations of the reality. There are ancient chroniclers, as well as an historical fact from the thirteenth century. In 1228, Stefan, the King of Serbia had deteriorating health. It was his desire to be tonsured as a monk. Nearing death, he called for his brother Sava to come to the capital of Ras. However, Sava arrived late, Stefan had already reposed. Sava then prayed to the Tri-Hypostatical Divinity to restore the nous of the King so that he might tonsure him and that the King might name his successor. The Tri-Hypostatical Divinity listened to Sava and returned the nous of Stefan. Stefan arose and spoke, naming Radislav, his eldest son, as successor. Then Sava garbed Stefan with the Angelic *Schema* of the monks and changed his name to Simon.[57] There is a significant difference, however, to the methodology utilized raising of the dead person. The Theanthropos does not pray but simply calls for Lazarus to come forth. The Theanthropos clearly shows He has the power to raise the dead within Himself.

Throughout the life of Jesus of Nazareth there are reactions to Miraculous Occurrences. This is confirmed from the Royal Record Office at Edessa. The historian, Eusebius checked the archives, including a letter from Jesus, and reports of the following. The archives confirm the Miraculous healing of King Abgar who was instantly cured of the disease and disorder from which he had suffered.[58]

Research confirms the scientific reason for the Tri-Hypostatical Divinity entering history as Jesus of Nazareth. It is extremely difficult for infinite and eternal life to make its way into the human nous, so

---

[57] *The Lives of the Monastery Builders of the Holy Mountain Athos*, Buena Vista, Holy Apostles Covenant, 1992, 177 and Nicholai Velimirovich, *The Life of St. Sava*, Crestwood, Saint Vladimir's Seminary Press, 1989, 105-107.

[58] Eusebius, *The History of the Church*, Toronto, Penguin Books Canada Ltd., 1989, 30-34.

narrow, and into the even narrower human body. Mankind is held behind bars since they are suspicious of anything coming from outside of their frame of reference. Mankind is cast into a prison of time and space unable – from atavism or perhaps from inertia – to bear being penetrated by something outlasting time, outlying space, something that surpasses these, and is eternal. Such an invasion is considered to be an aggression towards them, and they respond with war. He is given the fact that he is being corrupted by the "moth of time", does not like the intrusion of eternity into his life and is not easily able to adapt himself to it. He considers this intrusion to be sheer unforgivable insolence. Certain times mankind might become a hardened rebel against eternity because in the face of it an individual perceives his own minuteness, while at others he even experiences fierce hatred towards it because he views it through such a human prism, one that is all-too earthbound, all-too worldly. Since he is plunged bodily into matter, bound by the force of gravity to time and space his nous is quite divorced from eternity, so the world-weary man takes no pleasure in those arduous expeditions towards the eternal. The chasm existing between time and eternity is quite unbridgeable for him because he lacks the strength and ability needed to get across it. Thoroughly besieged by death, he covers with scorn all those who say to him that man is truly immortal and eternal. In order for a person to be immortal he must, at the very core of his sense of self, feel that he is immortal. For him to be immortal, in the centre of his consciousness, he must know himself eternal. Without doing this, both immortality and eternity alike will be conditions imposed from the outside. And if at one time he did have this sense of immortality and awareness of eternity, he had it so long ago that it has since wasted away under the weight of death, and waste away it really has. He learns this from the whole of his mysterious makeup. Our whole problem lies in how he might rekindle that extinguished feeling, how he might revive the wasted-away awareness. He is not in a position to do this; nor, indeed, are the "gods" of philosophy. The Tri-Hypostatical Divinity, Who incarnates His immortal Self inside mankind's sense of himself and incarnated His eternal Self within man's self-awareness, can only do this. Jesus does precisely this when He is made man and becomes the Theanthropos. Only in Jesus of Nazareth, in Him alone, does mankind feel that they are immortal and know that they are eternal. Jesus of Nazareth, the Theanthropos, bridges the chasm between time and eternity and restores relations between every one of them.[59]

Research confirms Jesus of Nazareth is the Theanthropos and is the Second Hypostasis of the Tri-Hypostatical Divinity. Jesus of Nazareth who is Man was once the Uncompounded. What He was He continues to be; what He was not He took to Himself. In the beginning He was, uncaused; for what is the cause of the Tri-Hypostatical Divinity. Afterward for a cause He is born, and that cause was that mankind might be saved, even those who insult Him and despise His being the Tri-Hypostatical Divinity. He took upon him mankind's denser nature, having conversed with flesh by means of mind. While His inferior nature, the humanity, became the Tri-Hypostatical Divinity, because it was united to the Tri-Hypostatical Divinity, and became one person because the higher nature prevailed in order that mankind too might be made god so far as He is made man. He is born – rather He is begotten: He is born of a woman – but she was a virgin. The first is human; the second, divine. In His human nature He has no father, but also in His divine nature – no mother. Both of these belong to the Tri-Hypostatical Divinity. He dwells in the womb – but He is recognized by the prophet, John the Baptist, himself still in the womb, leaping before the Word, for whose sake he came into being. He is wrapped in

---

[59] Popovich, 21-22

swaddling clothes – but He took off the swathing bands of the grave by His rising again. He was laid in a manger – but He is glorified by Ethereal Beings, and proclaimed by the Star, and worshiped by the Magi. Why does that which is presented to your sight, because you will not look at that which is presented to your mind, offend you? He is driven into exile into Egypt – but He drives away the Egyptian idols. He had neither form nor comeliness in the eyes of the Jews – but to David He is fairer than all the children of mankind. On the mountain He is bright as the lightning, and becomes more luminous than the sun, initiating us into the Mystery of the future. He is baptized as man – yet He remits sins as the Tri-Hypostatical Divinity – not because he requires purificatory rites Himself, but that He might sanctify the element of water. He is tempted as man, but He conquers as the Tri-Hypostatical Divinity; He bids us to be of good cheer for He has overcome the world. He hungered – yet He fed thousands; He is the bread that gives life, and that is of the Heavenly Realm. He thirsted – yet He cries, "If anyone thirsts, let him come to Me and drink."[60] He promises that fountains should flow from them that believe. He is wearied, but He is the rest for them that are weary and heavy-laden. He is heavy with sleep, but He walks lightly over the sea. He rebukes the wind; He makes Peter light as he began to sink. He pays tribute, but it is out of a fish; He is the King of those who demanded it. He is condemned as a Samaritan and demoniac, but He saves mankind that came down from Jerusalem and fell among thieves; the demonic Ethereal Beings acknowledge Him, and He drives them out, and sinks in the sea legions of foul spirits, and sees the prince of demonic Ethereal Beings falling like lightning. He is stoned yet is not taken. He prays, but He hears prayer. He weeps, yet He causes tears to cease. He asks where Lazarus was laid, for He is man; but He raises Lazarus, for He is the Tri-Hypostatical Divinity. He is sold,

---

[60] John 7:37

and very cheaply, for only thirty pieces of silver; yet He redeems the world, and that at a great price, for the price was His own blood. As a sheep He is led to the slaughter, but He is the Shepherd of Israel and now of the entire planet as well. As a lamb He is silent, yet He is the Logos. He is bruised and wounded; yet He heals every disease and infirmity. He is lifted up and nailed to the tree, yet by the Tree of Life He restores us; He saves even the robber crucified with Him; He wraps the visible world in darkness. He is given vinegar to drink mingled with gall. He turns the water into wine, Who is the destroyer of the bitter taste, Who is sweetness and altogether desired. He lays down His life, but He has Power to take it again; and the veil is rent, for the mysterious doors of the Heavenly Realm are open; the rocks are cleft, the dead arise. He dies, but He gives life, and by His death destroys death. He is buried but He rises again; He goes down into hell, yet He brings up the nous; He ascends to the Heavenly Realm and shall come again to Judge the living and the dead, and to put to the test such words as yours.[61]

Further research clarifies the relationship of Jesus of Nazareth as one Hypostasis in the Tri-Hypostatical Divinity.[62]

Jesus is called Son since He is identical with the Father in His Essence. He is called only begotten, not because He is the only Son and of the Father alone, and only a Son, but also because the manner of His Sonship is peculiar to Himself and not shared by bodies.

Jesus is called the Logos, because He is related to the Father as the Word to mind, not only on account of His passionless generation, but also because of the union, and of His declaratory function. The person who has mental perception of the Son has also perceived the Father; and the Son is a concise demonstration and easy setting forth of the Father's

---

[61] Gregory of Nazianzus cited by Edward R. Hardy, ed., *Christology of the Later Fathers*, Philadelphia, The Westminster Press, 1954, 173-175.
[62] The following research comes from Gregory of Nazianzus in his *The Theological Orations*. The research ends at the reference 11.

nature. Everything that is begotten is a silent word of Him that begot Him. Anyone can say that this name was given Him because He exists in all things that are, He would not be wrong. For what is there that exists but by the Word? He is also called Wisdom, as the knowledge of things divine and human. For how is it possible that He who made all things should be ignorant of the reasons of what He has made? He is Power as the only One Who sustains all of created things, and the finisher to them of Power to keep them together.

Jesus is the Truth, as being in nature one and not many, for truth is one and falsehood is manifold, and as the pure Seal of the Father and His most unerring impress. He is the Image, as of one substance with Him, and because He is of the Father, and not the Father of Him. For this is of the nature of an image, to be the reproduction of its archetype, and of that whose name it bears – only that there is more here. For in ordinary language an image is a motionless representation of that which has motion; but in this case it is the living reproduction of the living one and is more exactly like than any son to his father. For such is the nature of simple existences that it is not correct to say of them that they are like in one particular and unlike in another; but they are a complete resemblance and should rather be called identical than like. Moreover, He is called Light, as being the brightness of the nous cleansed by word and life. For if ignorance and sin were darkness, knowledge and godly life will be light.

Jesus is called Life since He is Light, and is the constituting and creating Power of every reasonable soul, "for in Him we live and move and have our being, as also some of your own poets have said, 'For we are also His offspring'"[63] according to the double Power of that breathing into us; for we were all inspired by Him with breath, and as

---

[63] Acts 17:28

many of us as were capable of it, and in so far as we open the mouth of our mind, with the Holy Spirit.

Jesus is righteousness since He distributes according to that which we deserve, and is a righteous arbiter both for those who are under the law and for those who are under grace, for nous and body, so that the former should rule, and the latter obey, and the higher have supremacy over the lower; that the worse may not rise in rebellion against the better.

Jesus is sanctification, as being purity, that the pure may be contained by purity. He is redemption, since He sets us free who were held captive under sin, giving Himself a ransom for us, the sacrifice to make expiation for the world. He is resurrection, because He rises up from hence, and brings to life, again us who were slain by sin.

These names, however, are still common to Him Who is above us, and to Him Who came for our sake. But others are peculiarly our own and belong to that nature which He assumed. So He is called man, not only that through His body He may be apprehended by embodied creatures, whereas otherwise this would be impossible because of His incomprehensible nature; but also that by Himself He may sanctify humanity, and be as it were a leaven to the whole lump; and by uniting to Himself that which is condemned may release it from all condemnation, becoming for all men all things that we are, except sin – body, nous, mind, and all through which death reaches – and thus He became man, who is the combination of all these; the Tri-Hypostatical Divinity in visible form, because He retained that which is perceived by mind alone. He is son of man, both on account of Adam, and of the Virgin from whom He came: from the one as a forefather, from the other as his mother, both in accordance with the law of generation, and apart from it. He is Christ because He is the Tri-Hypostatical Divinity. For this is the anointing of His manhood, and does not, as in the case with all other anointed ones, sanctify by its action, but by the presence in His fullness of the anointing one; the effect of which is that that which anoints is called man, and makes that which is anointed the Tri-Hypostatical Divinity.

Jesus is the Way, because He leads us through Himself; the door, as letting us in; the Shepherd, as making us dwell in a place of green pastures, and bringing us up by waters of rest, and leading us there, and protecting us from wild beasts, converting the erring, bringing back that which was lost, binding up that which was broken, guarding the strong, and bringing them together in the fold beyond, with words of pastoral knowledge. The sheep, as the victim; the lamb, as being perfect; the high priest, as the one who offers; Melchizedek, as without mother in that nature which is above us, and without father in ours; and without genealogy above for whom, it says, shall declare his generation and, moreover, as King of Salem, which means peace, and King of Righteousness, and as receiving tithes from patriarchs, when they prevail over powers of evil. These are the titles of Jesus of Nazareth. Walk through them, those that are lofty in a godlike manner; those that belong to the body in a manner suitable to them; or rather, altogether in a godlike manner, that you may become a god, ascending from below, for His sake who came down from on high for ours. In all and above all keep to this, and you shall never err, either in the loftier or the lowlier names; Jesus is the same yesterday and today in the incarnation, and the Spirit forever and ever.[64]

The reality of the life of Jesus of Nazareth is among the best documented in history. The great celebration throughout the Earth was an acknowledgement of the greatness of this Person, since it was the two thousandth anniversary of the Nativity of Jesus of Nazareth. No mere man has had this kind of impact upon the Earth.

---

[64] Gregory of Nazianzus, *The Theological Orations*, which is cited by Hardy, 190-193

Jesus of Nazareth, as Theanthropos, is the most valuable of all beings and as such He is at the same time the highest criterion of all true values. In this world any inferior to the Theanthropos cannot become the criterion of all values because that which is of the greatest value is none other than the Theanthropos Himself. Man cannot be the criterion since his value is much less than that of the Theanthropos. The Theanthropos constitutes the highest criterion of anything divine or human both in this world and the next simply because He is the most valuable of all beings. History does not know a greater God than Jesus of Nazareth, or a greater man than Jesus of Nazareth. Jesus of Nazareth has revealed both simultaneously and completely God and man. Therefore, there is no God without the Theanthropos and there is no man without Theanthropos.

"What is truth?" inquired Pilate of the incarnate Truth, wanting to hear with his own ears that which he did not perceive with his eyes, as though it was not the same soul that was hearing through his ears and seeing through his eyes. Jesus of Nazareth is the Truth, not as word, neither as teaching nor as concrete energy, but as a most perfect and eternally living Theanthropic Hypostasis. It is only as a Theanthropic Personality that He is the criterion of Truth. It is for this reason that Theanthropos said "I am the way, the truth"[65] that is, He is the way to Truth itself, the criterion of Truth Himself, the essence of Truth itself. The criterion of Truth is the Truth itself, and the Truth is Theanthropos. Thus, whatever does not come from Him is not from the Truth. The Truth cannot ontologically exist outside of His Theanthropic Personality.

Truth is not a philosophical concept, nor is it a theory, a teaching, or a system, but rather, it is the living Theanthropic Hypostasis – the historical Jesus of Nazareth. Before Him men could only conjecture

---

[65] John 14:6

about the Truth since they did not possess Him. With Him as the incarnate divine Logos the eternally complete divine Truth enters into the world. For this reason the Gospel says: "truth came through Jesus Christ."[66]

What is life, real true life, and what is the criterion of life? It is none other than the Hypostasis of the Theanthropos. It is the Hypostasis and not merely His teachings separated from His miraculous and life-giving Hypostasis. On account of humanity's inescapable mortality no man has ever dared to say: I am the life. The Theanthropos does say, "I am ... the life."[67] He said this justifiably since He conquered death by His Resurrection and showed Himself to be eternally alive by His Ascension and through Him being placed at the right hand of the Father. For this reason, the Theanthropos is also the Life and the criterion of Life. What does not come from Him is dead. In Him life finds its rationality and its reasonableness because it finds its divine eternity. As the eternal divine Logos He is both life and all-life since life is only life through Him. Wherever one does not find Him, there one will find life transformed into death, because it is He alone who makes life really life. Rebellion from Him who is life always ends in mortality and death. It is for this reason that only in Him, as the Logos and the Reason of life, can one find the only possible rational justification for the existence of life in the category of time and space.

Eternal life is nourished and preserved through the eternal good, justice, truth, wisdom, and light. When the Theanthropos proclaims: "I am the Life," He is also proclaiming the following: I am the Good, I am the Justice, I am the Truth, I am the Wisdom, and I am the Light. Since then, He is all of these simultaneously; He is also the criterion of all of these. By His most perfect personality, the sinless Theanthropos

---

[66] John 1:17
[67] John 14:6

constitutes for mankind the only infallible criterion of life, goodness, justice, truth, wisdom, and light. The Theanthropos is the highest and most perfect being, the only eternal being and therefore the highest and most perfect criterion, the only eternal criterion, of truth, life, justice, light, goodness, and wisdom.[68]

The reality of the Theanthropos is confirmed by the following Ecumenical Councils. The Third Ecumenical Council calls Jesus of Nazareth perfect God and perfect man, composed of a rational nous and body, consubstantial to us according to His humanity. The Fourth Ecumenical Council decrees that we confess one and the same Christ, Son, Lord, Only Begotten; acknowledged in two natures without confusion, change, division or separation; the difference of the natures being in no way removed because of the union, but rather the property of each nature being preserved and both concurring into one Person and one Hypostasis. Although He possesses two natures, the divine and human, which are inseparably and indivisibly united, Christ is still but one person and not two. The Sixth Ecumenical Council adds, we confess in the one and the same Christ two natures and two natural operations (i.e., energies) indivisibly, inconvertibly, inseparably and unconfusedly; and two natural wills, not contrary to one another, but His human will follows the divine neither resistingly nor reluctantly, but rather as subject to His divine and omnipotent will."[69]

This confirms that Jesus of Nazareth is the Truth since He is the Theanthropos Who is the Second Hypostasis of the Tri-Hypostatical Divinity. Historical and corroborating proofs have been provided.

The reality is that seeking the Truth produces Disciples and this is scientifically verifiable. The Truth is not a concept. The Truth is one

---

[68] Popovich, 77-79.
[69] Frangopoulos, 136

Hypostasis of the Tri-Hypostatical Divinity. Christology proves this reality of the Theanthropic Ethical category.

New Data:

There is new scientific research that is based on forensic data that is quite exciting to me. J. Warner Wallace utilizes his knowledge of forensic science as a cold case detective to prove Christological conclusions. His book, *Person of Interest*,[70] he explains "why Jesus matters in a world that rejects the Bible". This confirms that the co-called "BCE" (Before the Common Era) and "CE" (Common Era) are not technically correct. They should be technically "B.C." (Before Christ) and A.D, (Anno Domini - in the year of the Lord) which is placed before the date. The book also confirms

I finally came upon an exceptional scientifically verifiable book on Christology in English! There are numerous books dealing with Christology, yet only one, so far, in English. Saint Nektarios book is an exceptional Christological addition utilizing unique methodologies to answer previous questionable scientific questions. For example, in seminary the position was that Christ was born in 6 B.C. and died AD 33, when He was 33 years old! My query was based on the fact 33 + 6 did not equal 33? Nektarios utilized the Greek and Roman chronology to show that Christ's Ministry commenced in 785 AUC (Ab urbe condita).[71] There are numerous Christological books awaiting translations into the English language.

There is a self-portrait that Christ made for King Abgar of Edessa who suffered from a malady:

---

[70] J. Warner Wallace, *Person of Interest*. Grand Rapids, Zondervan Reflective, 2021.
[71] Nektarios, *Christology*, 217-219

Angelology

Angelology is the study of Ethereal Beings. The first scientist, Enoch[72] wrote about Ethereal Beings, as a result of his acquaintance with them. Ethereal Beings assisted Enoch in much of his scientific research.

Enoch learned the Truth from the Ethereal Beings and was consequently honoured by the Tri-Hypostatical Divinity to continuously live in the Heavenly Realm.[73]

Some of Enoch's research has been disputed through demonic Ethereal Beings having conjugal relation with women. This may be a misunderstanding of the capacity of a male being possessed by a Demonic Ethereal Being. In these cases, even observed today, the man can provide sperm to impregnate the woman. The child's disposition would be to do harm.

Archaeological research confirms the sophistication of the Antediluvian Age, so it is important not to dismiss Enoch's research.

---

[72] This is *The Book of Enoch*, published by Clarendon Press, Oxford, 1912. This is disputed in some areas but is regarded as a Canonical Book by the Ecclesiastical National Community of Ethiopia. This is now available in English in Her Scripture: Ethiopian Bible in English Complete, Blue Nile Spiritual Texts, 2024.

[73] Symeon the New Theologian, *The First-Created Man*, Platina, St. Herman of Alaska Brotherhood, 1994, 117

This was an era where Ethereal Beings communicated directly with mankind.

Ethereal Beings are created first by the Tri-Hypostatical Divinity as a hierarchy. Ethereal Beings are called to perfect union with the Tri-Hypostatical Divinity through cooperative agreement of created will with the Will of the Tri-Hypostatical Divinity.[74] Ethereal Beings are created prior to time, in a non-temporal mode of existence.[75] Ethereal Beings are created uniquely, that is, in silence.[76] Ethereal Beings are now eternally divided into those that have unwavering attachment to the Truth and demonic Ethereal Beings that have eternal enmity to the Truth.[77]

All Ethereal Beings are embodied and circumscribable when compared to the Tri-Hypostatical Divinity Who is completely immaterial and bodiless. Compared with mankind Ethereal Beings are bodiless, invisible, and impossible to hold.[78]

Ethereal Beings are incapable of prophesying; there is no understanding of Cosmic Eschatology.[79]

Ethereal Beings are assigned as Guardians of each country.[80]

Ethereal Beings chant praises to the Tri-Hypostatical Divinity at the Ecclesiastical Temples during the Divine Liturgy in the Heavenly Realm and on Earth.[81]

---

[74] Vladimir Lossky, *The Mystical Theology of the Eastern Church*, Crestwood, St. Vladimir's Seminary Press, 1957, 97
[75] Ibid, 102
[76] Ibid, 107
[77] St. Basil the Great cited by Lossky, 102-103
[78] Symeon, *Ethical*, Vol. 1, 39-40
[79] Ibid, 71
[80] Ibid, 90
[81] Ibid, 177

All of the hierarchies of Ethereal Beings have one thing in common. They are androgynous.[82]

By their nature, Ethereal Beings are active spirits who have intelligence, will, and knowledge. They serve the Tri-Hypostatical Divinity, fulfill His Providential Will, and glorify Him. They are fleshless spirits and, in so far as they belong to the invisible world, our bodily eyes cannot see them. Ethereal Beings surpass mankind by their spiritual powers; however, they also, as created beings, bear in themselves the seal of limitation. Being fleshless, Ethereal Beings are less dependent than mankind on space and place, and so-to-speak, pass through vast spaces with extreme rapidity, appearing wherever it is required for them to act. Ethereal Beings are not omnipresent.[83] In other words, Ethereal Beings contain a nous and intelligence.[84]

Through adhering to the Truth, Ethereal Beings have obtained unfailing gladness and enjoyment.[85]

Ethereal Beings are divided into three hierarchical orders. The first hierarchy that is closest to the Tri-Hypostatical Divinity consists of Seraphim, Cherubim, and Thrones. The second hierarchy consists of Dominions, Powers, and Authorities. The third hierarchy, closest to physical creatures, consists of Rulers, Archangels, and Angels.[86]

Demonic Ethereal Beings, at their creation, were free and immaterial Ethereal Beings who misused their freedom to become evil. They were overcome by arrogance and pride, and under the leadership of Lucifer revolted against the Tri-Hypostatical Divinity. The Tri-Hypostatical

---

[82] This clarifies some abundant misconceptions in *The Holy Bible* and some interpretations. There is no possibility of bestiality.

[83] Michael Pomazansky, *Orthodox Dogmatic Theology*, Platina, Saint Herman of Alaska Brotherhood, 1984, 114-115

[84] Hierotheos of Nafpatkos, *Orthodox Psychotherapy*, Levadia, Birth of the Theotokos Monastery, 1995, 104, 203

[85] Symeon, <u>*Ethical*</u>, Vol. 1, 155-156

[86] Frangopoulos, 93

Divinity cast Lucifer and the rebellious Ethereal Beings into Hades. The Ethereal Beings became demonic, while Lucifer became the Devil, or Satan.[87]

Historical data provides proof that Ethereal Beings have become demonic. It was a very ancient opinion, that there are certain wicked and malignant demonic Ethereal Beings, which envy good people, and endeavour to hinder them in the pursuit of virtue; for fear that they should be partakers of greater happiness than they enjoy.[88] Satan is the chief among demonic Ethereal Beings, superior because it is an intellectual being, not subject to the body. The body is a lower element; consequently, it is superior. However, mankind is going to get that which Satan lost, that is, Paradise and the Heavenly Realm. This is why Satan is infuriated. Human psychology understands the root cause of Satan's fury. Just realize, Satan had immortal life, and it knew that it was damned. Then there is another being that is lower than it, that is mankind, who is not worth even spitting on, and he is going to get that which Satan lost. Of course, Satan is going to be terribly envious, because there is no repentance for it.[89]

Demonic Ethereal Beings are permitted to inhabit the aerial realm, the chief function being to frighten and tempt mankind in the hope of preventing them from becoming Disciples.[90]Researchers, such as Dr.

[87] Ibid, 96- 97

[88] Plutarch cited in Lewis Sperry Chafer, *Systematic Theology*, Grand Rapids, Kregel Publications, 1976, II, 37.

[89] Seraphim Rose, *Genesis, Creation and Early Man*, Platina, Saint Herman of Alaska Brotherhood, 2000, 488.

[90] Seraphim Rose, *The Soul After Death*, Fourth Ed., Platina, Saint Herman of Alaska Brotherhood, 1980, 28

Raymond Moody,[91] Dr. Robert Crookall,[92] Dr. Elizabeth Kubler-Ross,[93] and Robert Monroe have presented their findings on what is observed by people who have died and subsequently returned.

Robert Monroe has documented his visits to Satan's domain. Upon Satan's arrival there is no awestruck prostration or falling down on one's knees, it is rather, an attitude most matter of fact. It is an occurrence to which all are accustomed and to comply takes absolute precedence over everything else. There are no exceptions. At the signal, each living thing lies down with head turned to one side so that one does not see Satan as he passes by. The purpose seems to be to form a living road over which he can travel. There is no movement, as he passes by. In the several times that the observer experienced this, everyone lies down with the others. At the time, the thought of doing otherwise was inconceivable. As Satan passes, there is a roaring musical sound and a feeling of radiant, irresistible living force of ultimate power that peaks overhead and fades in the distance. It is an action as casual as halting for a traffic light at a busy intersection or waiting at a railroad crossing when the signal indicates that a train is coming; one is unconcerned and yet feels unspoken respect for the power represented in the passing train. The event is very impersonal.[94]

Ethereal Beings are well known to mankind through their participation in death. Eschatological research indicates the reality of Tollhouses. Ethereal Beings meet the deceased and escort the nous upwards. Throughout this upward path vile demonic Ethereal Beings, meet the nous to bring specific accusations. Should the accusation prove

---

[91] Dr. Raymond A. Moody, Jr., *Life After Life*, Atlanta, Mockingbird Book, 1975, cited by Rose, *Soul*.

[92] Dr. Robert Crookall, *Out-of-the-Body Experiences*, Secacus, The Citadel Press, 1970, cited ibid.

[93] Dr. Elizabeth Kubler-Ross, *On Death and Dying*, New York, Macmillan Publishing Co., 1969, cited Ibid.

[94] Robert A. Monroe, *Journeys Out of the Body*, cited Ibid, 114, 117, 118

truthful, the Ethereal Beings who act as escorts will "pay" through the good done by the nous. The nous usually cringes behind the Ethereal Beings, hence the reason for the escorts. As the nous progresses to each Tollhouse the demonic Ethereal Beings are fiercer and more horrifying. If the nous is unable to secure passage through the Tollhouses, the demonic Ethereal Beings take them to Satan's abode. Should the nous successfully complete the passage through all of the Tollhouses their escorts take the nous to the Heavenly Realm. Tollhouses will be discussed more fully under Eschatology.[95]

Demonic Ethereal Beings are hideous, due to the rejection of the Grace that comes from the Theanthropos. By rejecting the Truth, darkness and unimaginable horrors result.[96] Demonic Ethereal Beings wish to destroy mankind through keeping them from acting on the Truth.[97]

The end result of following demonic Ethereal Beings is the death of the nous.[98] The descent toward this non-being is eternal. This is due to the reality that Ethereal Beings are eternal, yet the hatred toward the Tri-Hypostatical Divinity and His Will leads to an eternal descent to nothingness.[99]

Ethereal Beings are assigned to assist mankind. Research indicates that some are assigned as guardians. Sin is a stench, which drives our guardian Ethereal Being away. It is important to continuously entreat our guardians not to desert us because of our failure. Virtue is a fragrance, an aroma which attracts Ethereal Beings, who act as guardians of mankind. Fasting, for example, queen of the virtues because it cleanses the nous of the stench of sin and evil, gives joy to our Ethereal Beings as escorts.[100]

---

[95] Vasilios Bakogiannis, *After Death*, Katerini, Tertios Publications, 1995, 61-67

[96] Seraphim of Sarov, *Revelations of St. Seraphim of Sarov*, Paris, 1932, cited by Lossky, 129

[97] Symeon, *Ethical*, Vol. 1, 162-163

[98] Hierotheos, *Psychotherapy*, 118

[99] Lossky, 129

[100] Bakogiannis, 59.

Ethereal Beings have massive power to the extent that the Earth could be destroyed by only one of them.[101]

Just as Enoch[102] studies with Ethereal Beings, so every person has the capacity of learning from Ethereal Beings in their opposition to demonic Ethereal Beings. This is the reality of life!

The Truth is learned from numerous sources, including Ethereal Beings. Judgment has divided Ethereal Beings into seekers of the Truth who have a joyous life in the nous and seekers of evil that become sickening wishing death to their nous.

The Truth provides peace and joy.

The Ethereal Beings in Council:

---

[101] Seraphim of Sarov, cited by Lossky, 129

[102] Further proof can be found in the *Ethiopian Bible in English Complete*, Blue Nile Spiritual Texts, 2024, 212-232.

CHAPTER

5

Anthropology

Anthropology is the scientific study of mankind. Anthropology is generally acknowledged as a discipline which studies mankind relating to concepts describing matters, such as biological systems and customs. This is extremely important for empirical theologians.

Anthropology, in this context, is the scientific study of mankind in relation to the Tri-Hypostatical Divinity.

The theory of evolution is a working supposition since research continues. However, many theologians and ethicists reject the theory of evolution as speculation, conjecture, and assumption.[103] There are increasing signs, however, that many other scientific disciplines are rejecting the theory. For instance, in the 1980's geologists began to challenge the reigning uniformitarian model demonstrating that it was incapable of accounting for the rock beds of the earth's crust, especially the fossil deposits.[104] In 1997 an Israeli biophysicist and expert on the genetic code, spent thirty years researching the possibility of evolution on the genetic level. He not only shows why random mutations will never produce what the theory hypothesises but offers new scientific

---

[103] Chafer, II, 130
[104] Rose, *Genesis*, 36

avenues for investigating how variation occurs within the strict genetic limits of each kind of organism.[105]

Without the awareness of mankind's original nature, mankind cannot know what it is that we are striving to get back to; we cannot understand why we were created. Adam was in a state of nipsis. He saw everything as it truly was. Research indicates that people have returned to this same state of nipsis, with pure, open awareness. They perceive the original nature of mankind, with the distinct natures of all creation, through the Creative Mind of the Tri-Hypostatical Divinity.[106]

Man is created as the apex of the Tri-Hypostatical Divinity's creation. Man is created as a combination of earth and nous. Unlike the rest of creation which is spoken into existence by the Tri-Hypostatical Divinity, the first man is fashioned from the earth with his nous being breathed directly into him.[107] This makes mankind unique from anything else in creation.[108]

Mankind is created as monarch of the Earth with the highest of rights having dominion over all creatures.[109]

Mankind was originally united with the Tri-Hypostatical Divinity through communication yet had not attained his pure nature through theosis.[110]

Mankind lived originally in a Paradise, in the Garden of Eden. The Garden contains material bounties, such as exceptional fruit from innumerable trees for consumption, enjoyment, and nurturing. The Garden contains spiritual bounties through the presence of the

---

[105] Dr. Lee Spetner, *Not by Chance!*, cited by Rose, *Genesis*, 38
[106] Rose, *Genesis*, 46-47; Lossky, 120
[107] Frangopoulos, 99
[108] Gregory the Theologian, cited by Frangopoulos, 102
[109] Frangopoulos, 106
[110] Lossky, 126

Tri-Hypostatical Divinity and His Ethereal Beings for sweet fragrance and true happiness.[111]

Archaeologist David Rohl has documented his research in finding the Garden of Eden in a fascinating video. The research in indisputable.[112]

In the Garden of Eden there are two specific trees. There is the Tree of Knowledge and the Tree of Life. There is nothing unique about the Tree of Knowledge with the exception that there was a restriction placed upon eating the fruit of this one particular tree. Upon eating this fruit, evil becomes experiential for mankind. The Knowledge is that obedience is good while disobedience is evil.[113]

The Tree of Life is available to Adam and Eve until the Fall. The Tree of Life is available to Disciples today.[114] The Tree of Life is the Theanthropos. The leaves symbolize the most refined, exalted, with enlightened understanding of the Tri-Hypostatical Divinity's Decrees. The fruit symbolizes the Perfect Knowledge revealed in the Second Advent. The leaves also provide healing for Disciples who lack for nothing.[115]

The Tri-Hypostatical Divinity calls mankind to theosis, within the context of freedom. Man may accept or reject the Will of the Tri-Hypostatical Divinity. The image of the Tri-Hypostatical Divinity that is given to mankind is impossible to destroy.[116]

Freedom of choice is indicative of mankind's imperfection with reference to the Truth. Disciples understand the Truth, so it is not necessary to have choice.[117] Disciples are called to Unity with the

---

[111] Frangopoulos, 110-111

[112] The video "In Search of Eden" is found at https://www.youtube.com/watch?v=xVoggCHlwPw

[113] Ibid, 111-112

[114] Symeon, *Ethical*, Vol. 1, 27-28

[115] Brian Keen, **POWER Living** *Through Revelation*, Scarborough, The Ethics Institute, 2009, 273-274

[116] Lossky, 124

[117] Maximus the Confessor, cited by Lossky, 125

Tri-Hypostatical Divinity. This Unity is realization of perfect assimilation through Grace.[118]

The nous possesses logic, wisdom, and contains discernment. The earthly body is led by desires.[119] The temple of the body is the combination of the nous and earthly body which feeds on the Theanthropos' Body and Blood.[120] The Ecclesia provides the opportunity for the Image of the Tri-Hypostatical Divinity throughout mankind's hypostases, which produces true unity.[121]

Man is created in the image of the Tri-Hypostatical Divinity so that he can control nature through assimilation into the Archetype found in the Heavenly Realm. Consequently, the image is granted to all of mankind throughout creation.[122]

Eve's creation is also due to the direct intervention of the Tri-Hypostatical Divinity, since she comes directly from Adam's flesh and bone.[123] The flesh from Adam's side was replaced by the Tri-Hypostatical Divinity. As Eve, and all women, came from Adam's side and all mortal men come from her, so the Theanthropos, Jesus of Nazareth comes from the flesh of a woman. The Theanthropos takes flesh from the Virgin Mary to replace that which Adam had lost in Eve's creation.[124]

The Fall comes about due to mankind's inability to respond to the Truth. The Tri-Hypostatical Divinity calls Adam to repent of eating fruit from the Tree of Knowledge, but Adam makes an excuse.[125] The Tri-Hypostatical Divinity then calls Eve to repent of eating from the Tree of Knowledge, but she makes an excuse. Both refuse to acknowledge the

---

[118] Lossky, 125
[119] John Chrysostom, cited by Frangopoulos, 102
[120] Frangopoulos, 101
[121] Lossky, 120-121
[122] Ibid, 120
[123] Ibid, 123
[124] Symeon, *Ethical*, Vol. 1, 111
[125] Ibid, Vol. 1, 113

Truth and repent. Consequently, both of their nous dies leaving them naked and ashamed.[126]

Mankind is intelligent, seeking knowledge. For example, Enoch seeks to answer numerous questions, as any scientist would. Communing with Ethereal Beings is not unusual.

The nous is not un-begotten, uncreated, nor did it first exist in the unchanging world of ideas, but it is a creature, since it was created at a definite moment. The nous is immortal, but not because it existed before the body, nor because immortality is its natural quality, but because the Tri-Hypostatical Divinity willed it to be so. From the nous' creation the Tri-Hypostatical Divinity endowed the nous with immortality, that is to say, to have no end. Thus, immortality is a quality of the nous, but by Grace and not by nature. One cannot separate the nous from the body dialectically, since mankind is not a duality, but the whole of any person is made up of nous and body. The nous is not the whole of a person, but one portion. We find in the Mysteries of the Ecclesia the sanctifying of the whole person, who is made up of nous and body. Through the Resurrection of the Theanthropos the whole of every person, even the body, acquires the possibility of resurrection.[127]

After the Fall, the nous is confused, overcome by darkness and passions. The nous now suffers from this sickness. The result of dominating physical intelligence is a tremendous abnormality. The egotistical energies create arrogance which turns to raging abnormality.[128]

Mankind was originally created holy, passionless, and sinless in the image and likeness of the Tri-Hypostatical Divinity.[129] Research

---

[126] Symeon, *First-Created*, 91

[127] Hierotheos of Nafpaktos, *Life After Death*, Levadia, Birth of the Theotokos Monastery, 1996, 138-139

[128] Hierotheos, *Psychotherapy*, 206-207

[129] Enoch; and Symeon *First-Created*.

indicates that people may neither naturally see through their physical eyes nor think through their physical brain.[130]

Creatures were submissive until the Fall of Creation. Then all of the creatures no longer wished to submit to mankind. The relationship of animosity between mankind and creatures continued to grow until the Theanthropos comes and brings the Ecclesia into time.[131]

The ancestral sin of Adam and Eve, with all of its consequences, was passed on through natural birth to all their offspring, that is, to all of mankind. The consequence of being a person is that everyone is born already sinful and under all the consequences of sin: sorrow, illness, and death. Thus, the consequences of the Fall of Creation into sin turns out to be enormous and heavy. Mankind is deprived of the blessed life of Paradise in the Garden of Eden. The Earth, darkened by sin, was changed. The Earth from that time began to produce a harvest only with much labour. In fields, instead of good fruit, weeds grow; animals begin to fear mankind, to become wild, seeking prey. Illness, suffering, and death appear. Most importantly, mankind, through sinfulness, loses the very close and direct communion with the Tri-Hypostatical Divinity. The Tri-Hypostatical Divinity no longer appears to people visibly, as in Paradise, and every person's prayers become imperfect.[132]

Mankind's sense of unity in Truth is shattered as a result of the Fall. Individualism enters with the resultant reality that the husband (as head) and wife relationships develop.[133]

Sin is a disease of the will, which ceases to recognize the Truth.[134]

[130] Dr. Elizabeth Kubler-Ross, "Death Does Not Exist," *The Co-Evolution Quarterly*, Summer 1977, pp. 103-104, cited by Fr. Seraphim Rose, *Soul*.
[131] Joanne Stefanatos, D.V.M., *Animals and Man: A State of Blessedness*, Minneapolis, Light and Life Publishing Company, 1992. This entire book shows examples of how confirmed Saints have reestablished their relationship with irrational creatures.
[132] Slobodskoy, 107
[133] Lossky, 123
[134] Gregory of Nyssa, cited by Lossky, 128

People die as a result of the nous separating from the earthy body.[135]

Mankind was taught evil by demonic Ethereal Beings.[136] Wickedness continued for a very long time becoming so widespread and pervasive that all of mankind showed very little of the seed of justice.[137]

Mankind in antiquity, for the course of many years, learned from one another through Tradition, and knew their Creator as the Tri-Hypostatical Divinity. Later, when mankind had multiplied and began to give their mind over from their youth to evil thoughts, they forgot the Tri-Hypostatical Divinity and their Creator, and began not only to worship demonic Ethereal Beings, but even to deify such creatures as had been given to serve them. From this mankind has allowed every impurity and defiled by their unclean works the earth, the air, the heaven, and everything under the heaven. Nothing so defiles and so makes impure the pure works of the hands of the Tri-Hypostatical Divinity as when someone begins to deify it.[138]

At the evil instigation of the envious tempter, mankind suffered what Satan had suffered. Satan sinned by overvaluing its worth and by desiring to erect its throne higher than the Throne of the Tri-Hypostatical Divinity. Mankind prompted by Satan (slayer of mankind and the inventor of lies) imagined great things about himself. Mankind was deceived to think that if he were to leave the Tri-Hypostatical Divinity he would receive greater benefits. But immediately he realized that he had lost even what he had, seeing the fearful forewarning of the Tri-Hypostatical Divinity "but of the tree of the knowledge of good and evil you shall not eat, for in the day that you eat of it you shall surely die."[139] This now becomes a reality. The misanthropic Satan with its

---

[135] Cyril of Jerusalem and Athanasius the Great, cited by Frangopoulos, 102

[136] Enoch

[137] Irenaeus of Lyons, *Proof of the Apostolic Preaching*, New York, Newman Press, 1952, 58

[138] Symeon, *First-Created*, 95.

[139] Genesis 2: 17

opposing advice poured like poison its own death bearing power upon mankind.[140]

The first scientist, Enoch continues to live. The metastasis of Enoch indicates that this decision is temporary, and that death will eventually be abolished. By taking Enoch, the Tri-Hypostatical Divinity notifies His creatures that the foundation of death is weak. He affirms that as sin is nourishment for death, so also is righteousness a refutation and a disappearance of death. The first spoil, death, received a righteous man, Abel, but another righteous man, Enoch, abolishes death. Enoch overcomes death and proves it to be impotent.[141]

We see in mankind's life today something of the very temptation that Adam had. Although Adam was not fallen then, and in this regard his state was different from our present state, nonetheless, his situation was similar to that of a young person of sixteen, seventeen or eighteen years of age who is brought up in goodness and then comes to the age when he must himself make a choice of whether to be good or not. It so happens that, because we have freedom, there must be choice. One must consciously will to do what is good. Sooner or later in freedom one must actively choose the good or else it does not become part of the person.[142]

Mankind incrementally allowed arrogance and pride to destroy his relationship with the Tri-Hypostatical Divinity. There was one language and one race of mankind. As a result of disobedience to the Truth, mankind separated from one progenitor to become many countries and races. Every person is a descendent of Adam and Eve.[143]

The Truth provides mankind the opportunity to become Disciples.

---

[140] Nikolaos P. Vassiliadis, *The Mystery of Death*, Athens, The Orthodox Brotherhood of Theologians, 1993, 69
[141] Ibid, 115
[142] Rose, *Genesis*, 174
[143] Frangopoulos, 103-104

This is our nature originally. Anthropological research indicates that mankind was originally predisposed to the Truth and Unity.

Disciples can understand the Truth and Unity since this is our original existence and this can be rediscovered through the Ecclesia.

New Data

There are at least 2 books of research based on the creation of the universe. One is by Leslie Wickman who wrote *God of the Big Bang*, which is based upon the affirmation of the Creator through modern scientific conclusions.[144]

Another is authored by Hugh Ross who wrote *Improbable Planet*, which relates to the probabilities necessary for humanity to live on the planet Earth.[145]

Enoch living on Earth who will refute the antichrist since he is still alive:

---

[144] Wickman, Leslie, *God of the Big Bang*, Brentwood: Worthy Books, 2015.

[145] Hugh Ross, *Improbable Planet*. Grand Rapigs: Baker Books, 2016.

Hamartiology

Hamartiology is the study of the sickness[146] of sin and its consequences. This is extremely important within the scientific evaluation of health, and particularly within the context of medical science research.

All sin derives from one creature, namely, the Ethereal Being named Satan. Satan wages war against the Truth by assaulting mankind to follow evil.[147] Sin is a consequence of pride in exalting oneself against the Will of the Tri-Hypostatical Divinity.[148] The disease of sin leads to death.[149]

Egoism is the source of disunity.[150]

The topic of an unpardonable sin is greatly debated among theologians. To some, it is not even appropriate for today.[151] In all cases relating to the unpardonable sin, the reason why the forgiveness of sins is not possible is to be found in the sinners themselves, and not in the Will of the Tri-Hypostatical Divinity; more precisely, it lies in the lack of repentance on the part of people. Sin cannot be forgiven by the grace

---

[146] The term "sickness" is understood by the Ecclesia as a medical term. Refer to Hierotheos, *Psychotherapy*, 37

[147] Hierotheos, *Psychotherapy*, 218

[148] Frangopoulos, 114-115

[149] Symeon, *Ethical*, Vol. 2, 92-93

[150] Lossky, 121-122

[151] Chafer, II, 269

of the Holy Spirit, when blasphemy is spewed forth against this very grace. One must believe that, even in these sins, the sinners, if they offer sincere repentance and weep over their sins, they will be forgiven.[152]

The remedy for sin for mankind who are participants in the Eternal Organism, known as the Ecclesia, is to be empowered to diagnose their own troubles and apply intelligently the appropriate cure.[153] Although this has validity, the aspect of confession is appropriate for mankind psychologically. The Mystery of Repentance is discussed extensively in *The Forgotten Medicine*.[154] Satan, as we have seen under Angelology, is the initial source of sin.

The Ecclesia contains a pathological clinic to restrain the effects of sin. She calls all mankind to Perfection through the Truth.[155] The Ecclesia on Earth is not exempt from the challenge of the disease, since Her Believers and Faithful are still susceptible to this.[156]

Satan attacks those in the Ecclesia by asserting that their spiritual health is not due to the power of the Tri-Hypostatical Divinity. This is an appeal to the sin of pride.[157]

The Tri-Hypostatical Divinity continuously offers mankind the opportunity to repent of any wrongdoing. A perfect example is that of Enoch the first scientist. Enoch has not died as yet but was taken directly to the Heavenly Realm. He will return to refute the Antichrist. Had our first ancestors desired to repent even after the transgression of the commandment, then, even though they would not have restored to themselves what they had before the transgression of the commandment, at least they would have been delivered from the curses that were uttered

---

[152] Pomazansky, 290

[153] Chafer, II, 325

[154] Seraphim Aleksiev, *The Forgotten Medicine*, Wildwood, St. Xenia Skete Press, 1994.

[155] Hierotheos, *Psychotherapy*, 244

[156] Pomazansky, 244

[157] Symeon the New Theologian, *Homilies*, Homily 4, cited by Pomazansky, 265

to the earth and to themselves.[158] After the Fall of Creation, the Tri-Hypostatical Divinity gives Adam the opportunity to repent and be pardoned, but he remained unbending. For the Tri-Hypostatical Divinity comes and says to Adam, "Where *are* you?"[159] That is, from what glory into what shame have you come? And then, when He asks him why he sinned, why he transgressed, He prepared him especially so that he might say, "Forgive me." Yet there is no humility. There was no repentance, but the complete opposite. Adam contradicts and retorts, "The woman whom You gave *to be* with me"[160] deceived me. Adam does not say, "My wife deceived me," but "The woman whom You gave *to be* with me," as if to say that this misfortune is that which You have brought upon me.[161] Unfortunately, when man does not wish to reproach himself, he does not hesitate to accuse the Tri-Hypostatical Divinity Himself. Then the Tri-Hypostatical Divinity comes to Eve and says to her, in effect "Why did you not keep the commandment? He especially hinted to her, at least say, "forgive me," so your nous might be humbled and pardoned. But again, He did not hear the word "forgive." For she replies "The serpent deceived me,"[162] as if to say that the serpent sinned, and what is that to me? Repent, acknowledge your sin, have pity on your nakedness. Neither Adam nor Eve wishes to accept responsibility nor had the least humility. See how clearly to what our state has come, into what great misfortunes we have been led by the fact that we justify ourselves that we hold to our own will and follow ourselves.[163]

The effects of sin are extensive. Through sin, mankind opposes and fights the Tri-Hypostatical Divinity. Sin is the main energy of Satan because it can bear neither the Tri-Hypostatical Divinity nor anything

---

[158] Ephraim, cited by Rose, *Genesis*, 201
[159] Genesis 3:9
[160] Genesis 3:12
[161] Ephraim, cited by Rose, *Genesis*, 201
[162] Genesis 3:13
[163] Dorotheus of Gaza, cited by Rose, *Genesis*, 201-202

that is ethical. When Satan is firmly established in the *nous* of a person, it gradually destroys all goodness within him, first faith, then prayer, then love, fasting, and almsgiving. With the desire to sin, mankind is gradually planning suicide. The main task of the spiritually vigilant person is to kill the sin within himself, and, in this way, kill Satan, that attempts to assassinate us through sin.[164]

Through not acknowledging the reality of the Truth the philosophy of Nihilism has developed, and "relative truth" has arisen. Relative truth is always discursive, contingent, qualified, without category, with conclusions that can never be understood as an absolute. Let us consider the supposition: truth is relative. This is self-contradictory.[165]

We see that mankind has little in common with the first-created man, Adam when he lived in Paradise. Adam was immune to the action of the elements to such a degree that water could not drown him, fire could not burn him, the earth could not swallow him in its abyss, and the air could not harm him by any kind of action whatever. Everything was subject to him as the beloved of the Tri-Hypostatical Divinity, as the King and Lord of creation, and everything looked up to him, as the perfect crown of creatures."[166]

Mankind's sins are punished accordingly. Thus, it was fitting in all justice for the one who had become corruptible and mortal by reason of the transgression of the commandment, to live upon the corruptible earth and be nourished with corruptible food. Since a life without labour and an abundant food which grew by itself had caused him to forget the Tri-Hypostatical Divinity and the good things which He had given him and to disdain His commandment, he was therefore justly condemned to work the earth in the sweat of labour and in this way receive from it food little by little as from some kind of steward.

---

[164] Popovich, 199.

[165] Eugene Rose, *Nihilism*, Platina, St. Herman of Alaska Brotherhood, 2001, 12-13.

[166] Seraphim of Sarov, cited by Rose, *Genesis*, 188

The earth received the criminal after it had been cursed and had been deprived of its original productivity by which fruits were produced from it by themselves without labour. In order that it might be worked by him in sweat and labours and thus give him that little which it grows for his need, for the support of life, and if it will not be worked, to remain fruitless and to grow only thorns and thistles.[167]

The presence of sin and suffering is not the failure of the Tri-Hypostatical Divinity. These are the inevitable default and bankruptcy of Satan's lie. Though its ramifications seem to reach out to infinity, there is but one lie. The Tri-Hypostatical Divinity either rules over His universe, or He does not. The lie declares that He does not; the Truth declares that He does. Such a prodigious issue could not be treated with indifference.[168]

Through this sickness the unregenerate are susceptible to evil which has become the norm of the nous.[169] This is not normal for regenerate man.[170]

The consequence of the sickness is: an absolute alienation from the Tri-Hypostatical Divinity resulting in dishonesty; death of earthly body; darkening of the nous; guilt with resultant punishment; and the passage of the sickness to one's descendants.[171]

This sickness infects all of creation as a result of Adam's disobedience to the Tri-Hypostatical Divinity.[172] The nous becomes either bestial or demonic since this is opposition to the Laws of Nature, the Truth.[173]

The unregenerate exist in darkness since they are unable to exist in the presence of the Light of the Truth.[174]

---

[167] Symeon *First Created*, 92

[168] Chafer, II, 93

[169] Symeon, *Ethical*, Vol. 2, 80

[170] Ibid, 79-80

[171] Frangopoulos, 121-126

[172] Cyril of Alexandria, Commentary on Epistle to the Romans, PG 74, 788f, cited by Hierotheos, *Psychotherapy*, 37

[173] Gregory Palamas, Homily 51, 10, EPE 11, p. 114f, cited Ibid.

[174] Symeon, *Ethical*, Vol. 2, 96

The Light is produced by the Holy Flame of the Tri-Hypostatical Divinity Who destroys anything that is not Holy.[175]

The existence of education reveals the fact that mankind is an imperfect and incomplete being, as has been witnessed and continues to be witnessed from the experience of the human race. All philosophies, all religions, the sciences, and a myriad of civilizations testify to this fact. Mankind is a being that must be perfected and completed. Therefore, the main purpose of education is to perfect and to complete mankind. Observed from every side, mankind is, according to his essence, open towards other beings and to other worlds. He is in no way the closed monad of Leibnitz. With all his being, both his natural and psychic self, mankind weaves together, consciously or subconsciously, willing and instinctively, the enormous and incomprehensible net of life encompassing the whole world. Education, if it wants to be truly human, must begin from observable facts, as well as from fundamental logical principles. The existence in history of the search for what is perfect and complete gives birth in our conscience to the passionate question, who is a perfect and complete human being? Mankind considers people like Plato, Siddartha Gautama (known as Buddha), Moses, Mohammed, Kant, Shakespeare, Goethe, Tolstoy, and Nietzsche as potentially perfect. From the first to the last there is one sorrowful parade of imperfect and incomplete men. Yet in the middle of them stands That One who had the fullness of mystery, the wondrous Jesus of Nazareth, in a divine way perfect and humanly real (i.e., Theanthropos). As man His goodness is divinely perfect and complete. His human love is divinely perfect and complete; as is His righteousness, and His mercy, and His compassion, and His immortality, and His eternity and His beauty: all are humanly real but also divinely perfect and complete. Nothing is miraculous because He has transformed all things human

---

[175] Ibid, Vol. 2, 98-99

to divine. He has completed and perfected everything by the divine. In one word, the whole man in Him is divinely perfected and divinely completed. Try to imagine a more perfect God than the Theanthropos or a more perfect man than Him.[176]

Disciples utilize the Light of the Truth to learn every reality, including the Laws of Science. The Truth is available to all who wish the Wisdom of the Theanthropos.[177]

According to Eschatological research sin will be destroyed. The implications of this reality will be discussed under Eschatology.

The Truth is that the present inertia that mankind suffers from is a result of sin. Free Enterprise should be rewarded since this is one way to resolve this inertia.

The answer to all problems in ethics is unity through understanding the Truth. That is why hamartiology is an important subject to study. In attempting to find the Truth unity can be achieved for everyone. Even creation benefits from unity based upon the Truth.

There is a Judgment for every person

---

[176] Popovich, 5
[177] Symeon, *Ethical*, Vol. 2, 100-101

Soteriology

The importance of utilizing scientific methodologies is never more pertinent than in the area of Soteriology. Sadly, the most extensive proofs provided by Dr. Justin Popovich's research entitled *The God-Man and His Work: Christology and Soteriology* is still not presently available in English.[178]

Dr. Justin Popovich, 20th century theologian

---

[178] Daniel Rogich, *Serbian Patericon*, I, Platina, St. Herman of Alaska Brotherhood, 1994, 254

In its broadest significance, the concept of Soteriology includes every undertaking by the Tri-Hypostatical Divinity for the believer and the disciple from deliverance out of the lost estate to final Glory through deification.[179]

Research indicates that Soteriology is a function of the Theanthropos. The Holy Gospel quotes Jesus of Nazareth as saying, "The words that I speak to you are spirit, and *they* are life,"[180] for each one of them pours out from itself saving, sanctifying, grace-filled, life-creating, transfiguring power. Without the Truth of the Tri-Hypostatical Divinity, we have none of the Power of the Tri-Hypostatical Divinity on which mankind draws and which vivifies, sanctifies, and deifies. Without the Truth Who is the Theanthropos, there is no Soteriological component to mankind.[181]

There is proof relating to the three offices held by Jesus of Nazareth as the Theanthropos, namely: Prophet, Priest, and King of kings.

`The Theanthropos emphasizes the necessity of His teaching and observes that the true teaching and knowledge concerning the Tri-Hypostatical Divinity was hidden and unknown because of the madness of idolatry and atheism which had possessed the world. It was impossible for mankind to do so because everyone had been wounded and blinded by demonic deceit and the vanity of idols. Thus, it was necessary for the Logos to come Who sees the nous and the mind, who moves and has authority over all things within creation and is the Tri-Hypostatical Divinity and who as man dwelt among mankind so that from those works which the Lord accomplished through the body, they might know the Truth of the Tri-Hypostatical Divinity.[182]

The Priestly Office of the Theanthropos offered the sacrifice on

---

[179] Chafer, III, 6
[180] John. 6:63
[181] Popovich, 44
[182] Athanasius the Great, cited by Frangopoulos, 155

behalf of all, and in the place of all He gave up His Temple, that is His human nature, over to death. Now the Logos accepted Himself as the sentence for mankind and suffering in the flesh on behalf of all. He granted us infinite blessings of infinite value.[183]

The Theanthropos is the King of kings. There are numerous proofs relating to this. Confirming historical proof is provided in Chapter 3 – Christology. In addition, the magi recognized His right as King at His Nativity.[184] His Royal Dignity, however, is shown at its fullest during His descent into Hades. There He shattered and utterly annihilated the Kingdom of Hades and raised the dead who for centuries had been held there.[185]

The suffering of the Theanthropos is confirmed in research, such as His hanging upon a cross, which was the most disgraceful, agonizing, and cruel form of death penalty. In those times such a death penalty was imposed only on the most hardened criminals, such as thieves, murderers, instigators of rebellion, and felons. The torture of a crucified man is impossible to describe. Besides unbearable pain in every part of the body, the crucified person underwent the ordeal of terrible thirst and spiritual suffering until death. Death was so slow that many people suffered on the cross for several days. Even the executioners, who were habitually brutal, could not keep their composure while looking at the suffering of a crucified man. They prepared a beverage by which they tried to quench his unbearable thirst; or by adding various substances they tried to temporarily dull consciousness and alleviate the suffering. By the Law of Judaism, a crucified man was considered cursed. The

---

[183] Ibid, 158
[184] *The Life of the Virgin Mary, The Theotokos*, Buena Vista, Holy Apostles Convent, 1989, 201-218
[185] Frangopoulos, 159

leaders of Judaism at the time wanted to disgrace Jesus of Nazareth forever by condemning Him to such a death.[186]

There is research relating to the responsibility for the death of Jesus of Nazareth, the Theanthropos. Until His Advent into our terrestrial world, mankind knew only about death and death knew about mankind. Everything human was penetrated, captured, and conquered by death. Death was closer to mankind than anything else, and more powerful, incomparably more powerful than every man individually and all mankind together. The Earth was a dreadful prison of death, and people were the helpless slaves to death. Only with the Theanthropos was life manifested; eternal life appeared to hopeless mortals, wretched slaves of death. Through eternal life mankind has seen with their eyes, handled with their hands, and thus making manifest eternal life to all. For living in union with the Theanthropos, mankind can live eternal life here upon the Earth. Jesus of Nazareth is the Theanthropos and eternal life. He comes into the world to show all of mankind the Tri-Hypostatical Divinity and eternal life in Him. Genuine and true love for mankind consists of this, only of this; "God has sent His only begotten Son into the world, that we might live through Him"[187] and through Him live eternal life. "He who has the Son has life; he who does not have the Son of God does not have life."[188] He is completely in death. Life in the Theanthropos is really our only true life because it is wholly eternal and completely stronger than death. A life which is infected by death and which ends in death cannot really be called life. Just as honey is not honey when it is mixed with a poison, which gradually turns all the honey into poison, so a life, which ends in death, is not true life. There is no end to the Love of the Theanthropos for mankind because to acquire life eternal which is in Him, and to live by

---

[186] Slobodskoy, 354
[187] 1 John. 4:9
[188] 1 John. 5:12

Him, nothing is required of us not learning, nor glory, nor wealth, nor anything else that one of us does not have, but rather only that which each of us can have. That is faith in Jesus of Nazareth as Theanthropos. For this reason did He, the Only Friend of Man, reveal to mankind this wondrous good tiding, "For God so loved the world that He gave His only begotten Son, that whoever believes in Him should not perish but have everlasting life. He who believes in the Son has everlasting life."[189] As for the Tri-Hypostatical Divinity giving mankind what no Ethereal Being or human can give, the Theanthropos alone of all of mankind had the boldness and right to declare, "Most assuredly, I say to you, he who believes in Me has everlasting life"[190] and "but has passed from death into life."[191] Faith in Jesus of Nazareth unites mankind with the Tri-Hypostatical Divinity Who, according to the measure of each person's faith, pours out in his/her nous eternal life so that he/she then feels and realizes him/herself to be eternal. This he/she feels to a greater degree inasmuch as he/she lives according to faith, which gradually sanctifies his/her nous, heart, conscience, entire being, by the grace-filled energies of the Tri-Hypostatical Divinity. In proportion to the faith of a person the sanctification of his/her nature increases. The holier the person becomes, the stronger and more vivid is his/her feeling of personal immortality and the consciousness of his/her own and everybody else's immortality. Actually, a person's real life begins with his/her faith in Jesus of Nazareth as the Theanthropos, which commits all his/her nous, all his/her heart, all his/her strength to Him, Who gradually sanctifies, transfigures, and deifies him/her. Through the sanctification, transfiguration, and deification the grace-filled energies of the Tri-Hypostatical Divinity, which gives him/her the all-powerful feeling and consciousness of personal immortality and personal eternity,

---

[189] John 3:16, 36
[190] John 6:47
[191] John 5:24

are poured out upon him/her. In reality, every life is life inasmuch as it is in the Theanthropos. As much as it is in the Theanthropos is shown by its holiness, the holier a life, the more immortal and more eternal it is. Opposed to this process is death. Death is ripened sin; and ripened sin is separation from the Tri-Hypostatical Divinity, in Whom alone is life and the source of life. This Truth is evangelical and divine; holiness is life, sinfulness is death; piety is life, atheism is death; faith is life, unbelief is death; the Tri-Hypostatical Divinity is life, Satan is death. Death is separation from the Tri-Hypostatical Divinity, and life is returning to the Tri-Hypostatical Divinity and living in the Tri-Hypostatical Divinity. Faith is indeed the revival of the nous from lethargy, the resurrection of the nous from the dead, "I *am* He who lives, and was dead, and behold, I am alive forevermore. Amen. And I have the keys of Hades and of Death."[192] Mankind experiences this Resurrection of the nous from death for the first time with Jesus of Nazareth and constantly experiences it in His Ecclesia, since all of Him is found in Her. And He gives Himself to all of the Disciple through the Holy Mysteries and the holy virtues, Where He is, there is no longer death, there one has already passed from death to life. With the Resurrection mankind celebrates the deadening of death, the beginning of a new, eternal life. True life upon the Earth indeed begins from the Resurrection, for it does not end in death. Without the Resurrection human life is nothing else but a gradual dying which finally and inevitably ends in death. Real true life is that life which does not end in death. Such a life becomes possible upon the Earth only with the Resurrection of the Theanthropos. Life is real life only in the Tri-Hypostatical Divinity, for it is a holy life and by virtue of this an immortal life. Just as sin is death, so holiness is immortality. Only with faith in the Resurrection does mankind experience the most

---

[192] Revelation 1:18

crucial miracle of his existence, the Pascha from death to immortality, from being transitory into eternity, from hell to the Heavenly Realm. Only then does mankind find himself, his true self, his eternal self: "for this my son was dead and is alive again; he was lost and is found."[193] [194]

The sacrifice of the Theanthropos confirms the supposition of omniscience and the wisdom, which results from omniscience of the Tri-Hypostatical Divinity.

The Theanthropos has granted the soteriological reality by virtue of His substitution for mankind. There is sufficient historical proof to understand the Fall of Creation and mankind. The Theanthropos has made it possible for mankind to return to his/her natural state. Research indicates that one negative aspect of the theory of evolution is the attempt to overturn the position of Soteriology. The choice of evolution or intrusion applies to the redemption of mankind just as it does to the origin of life. Mankind requires a Saviour. According to its own philosophy, evolution eliminates the need for an extra-cosmic intelligence to intrude into human history, as happened when the Tri-Hypostatical Divinity becomes Jesus of Nazareth. Evolution itself has become a kind of saviour.[195]

Soteriology should begin by studying the Fall of Creation through mankind and his/her resurrection, which took place in the Theanthropos. This is very important, to look more broadly at the subject. It is important also because the subject of the Fall and Resurrection of Creation is the basis of Soteriology. If we do not examine it scientifically, we shall never be able to understand and live the life, which the Ecclesia has. The question of what the Fall is has been analysed in other books. One can find extensive analysis in the book *Orthodox Psychotherapy*.[196] The

---

[193] Luke 15:24
[194] Popovich, 32-35
[195] Rose, *Genesis*, 557
[196] Hierotheos, *Psychotherapy*

Fall of Creation is usually considered in juridical terms. The Ecclesia regards sin as an illness of mankind. Mankind fell ill and this illness had an effect on the whole human race.[197]

Research also regards the reality of redemption, as a result of Soteriology. Without the Truth of the Theanthropos, there is no salvation for mankind, for from it, when it is lived by a person, wells forth the saving power, which saves from sin, death, and Satan. This Truth about the Theanthropos, the lives of countless Saints most evidently and experientially bear witness to it. For the Saints are Saints by virtue of the fact that they constantly maintain Theanthropic lives as the nous of their nous, as the conscience of their conscience, as the mind of their mind, as the being of their being, as life of their life. Each one of them together with the Episcopate Paul may loudly proclaim the Truth, "it is no longer I who live, but Christ lives in me".[198] Delve into the Lives of the Saints, from all of them wells forth the grace-filled, life-creating, and saving power Who leads them from struggle to struggle, from virtue to virtue, from victory over sin to victory over death, from victory over death to victory over Satan, and leads them up into spiritual joy, beyond which there is no sadness, nor sighing, nor sorrow, but rather everything is only "peace and joy in the Holy Spirit"[199] joy and peace from the victory obtained over all sins, over all passions, over all deaths, over all demonic Ethereal Beings. All this, without doubt, is the practical and living testimony to the Dogma concerning the Most Holy Theotokos, truly more honourable than the Cherubim and beyond compare more glorious than the Seraphim, the Dogma which the Saints by faith carry in their hearts and by which they live with zealous love. Again, if you want one, two, or thousands

---

[197] Hierotheos of Nafpaktos, *The Mind of the Orthodox Church*, Lavadia, Birth of the Theotokos Monastery, 1998, 142-143

[198] Galatians 2:20

[199] Romans 14:17

of irrefutable testimonies of the life-bearing and life-creating nature of the All-Venerable Cross, and with this an experiential confirmation of the all-truthfulness of the holy Dogma of the saving nature of the Saviour on the Cross, then start out with the faith through the Lives of the Saints. You will have to feel and see that each Saint individually, and to all the Saints together, the power of the Cross is the all-vanquishing weapon with which they conquer all visible and invisible enemies of their salvation. The Cross in all their being, in their nous, in their heart, in their conscience, in their mind, in their will, and in their body, and in each one of them you will find an inexhaustible wellspring of the saving, all-sanctifying power which unfailingly leads them from perfection to perfection, and from joy to joy, until finally it leads them into the eternal Heavenly Kingdom where there is the unceasing triumph of those who keep festival and the infinite delight of those who behold the ineffable beauty of the face of the Tri-Hypostatical Divinity. Not only these aforementioned Dogmas are witnessed by the Lives of the Saints, but all the other Dogmas of the Ecclesia, of grace, of the Holy Mysteries, of the holy virtues, of mankind, of sin, of the holy relics, of the holy icons, of life beyond the grave, and of everything else which makes up the Theanthropic economy of salvation. The Lives of the Saints are experienced Dogmatics, experienced by the holy life of the holy people of the Tri-Hypostatical Divinity. In addition, in the Lives of the Saints is the Theanthropic Ethics in its entirety, Orthodox morality, in the full radiance of its Divine-human in all its sublime reality and its immortal life-creating nature. In them is shown and proven in a most convincing manner that the Holy Mysteries are the source of the holy virtues; that the holy virtues are the fruit of the Holy Mysteries, they are born of Them, they develop by Their help, they are nourished by Them, they live by Them, they are perfected by Them, they become immortal by Them, they live eternally by Them. All the Divine moral laws have their source in the Holy Mysteries and are realized in the holy virtues. For this reason, the Lives of the Saints are indeed experiential ethics that is applied ethics. The Lives of the Saints prove irrefutably that Ethics is nothing other than Applied Dogmatics. The entire Lives of the Saints have the Holy Mysteries and the holy virtues, and the Holy Mysteries and the holy virtues are gifts of the Holy Spirit Who accomplishes all in all. The Lives of the Saints are the only Orthodox pedagogical science.[200]

Further proof is provided in research related to reconciliation. In the Lives of the Saints are shown numerous but always certain ways of salvation, enlightenment, sanctification, transfiguration, theanthropic, deification; all the ways are shown by which mankind conquers sin, every sin; conquers passion, every passion; conquers death, every death; conquers the devil, every devil. There are countless nous-stirring examples of how a sinner becomes a righteous man in the Lives of the Saints, how a thief, a fornicator, a drunkard, a sensualist, a murderer, an adulterer, becomes a holy man. There are numerous examples of these in the Lives of the Saints, how a selfish, egotistical, unbelieving, atheistic, proud, avaricious, lustful, evil, wicked, depraved, angry, spiteful, quarrelsome, malicious, envious, malevolent, boastful, vainglorious, unmerciful, gluttonous man becomes a believer in the Tri-Hypostatical Divinity, in the Lives of the Saints.[201]

The judgment of the sin nature came through the Theanthropos' sacrifice on the Cross. Independent data confirming the crucifixion of Jesus of Nazareth being a true sacrifice is provided. From the hour that Jesus was crucified, from about 12 o'clock noon, the sun darkened, and there was darkness over the whole land until three o'clock in the afternoon, until He gave up His Spirit. Pagan historians,

---

[200] Popovich, 44-47
[201] Ibid, 48-49.

the Roman astronomer Flegontus and Junius Africanus noticed this remarkable, worldwide darkness. A noted philosopher from Asia, Dionysius the Aeropagite, in Egypt in the city of Heliopolis at the time, observed the sudden darkness and said, "Either the Creator is suffering or the world is coming to an end."[202]

The life in the Theanthropos originates in this life and arises from it. It is perfected, however, in the life to come, when mankind shall have reached that last day. It cannot attain perfection in man's souls in this life, nor even in that which is to come without already having begun here. "Now this I say, brethren, that flesh and blood cannot inherit the kingdom of God; nor does corruption inherit incorruption"[203] it casts a shadow over life in this present time. Therefore Paul thought it to be a great advantage to depart in order to be with Christ, for he says, "For I am hard-pressed between the two, having a desire to depart and be with Christ, *which is* far better."[204] But if the life to come were to admit those who lack the faculties and senses necessary for it, it would avail nothing for their happiness, but they would be dead and miserable living in that blessed and immortal world. The reason is, that the light would appear and the sunshine with its rays with no eye having been formed to see it. The Holy Spirit's fragrance would be abundantly diffused and pervading all, but man would not know it without already having the sense of smell. Now it is possible for the Theanthropos to make His friends to share in His Mysteries in preparation for that day, and for them to learn from Him what He has heard from God the Father, as He says, "No longer do I call you servants, for a servant does not know what his master is doing; but I have called you friends, for all things that I heard from My Father I have made known to you."[205] They

---

[202] Slobodskoy, 356.
[203] 1 Corinthians 15:50
[204] Philippians 1:23
[205] John 15:15

must come as His friend who "has ears to hear, let him hear!"[206] As the Theanthropos states in His parable, it is to prepare the wedding garment and to be ready with the other requisites for that bridal chamber; it is this life, which is the workshop for all these things. Those men who have not acquired these things before they departed have nothing in common with that life. To this the five foolish virgins and the man invited to the wedding feast are witnesses, since they came without either oil or the wedding garment and were not able to buy them then.[207]

There is an opportunity for not only individuals, but also for countries and Nations to experience Soteriological existence. When the Jewish people, which was called Israel, for this is the portion which is from the man's side, transgressed the commandment given to it by the Tri-Hypostatical Divinity, "Hear, O Israel: The LORD our God, the LORD *is* one"[208] when it had transgressed this and worshipped demons, and bowed to idols, and had eaten of their libations and sacrifices, then from it in turn as from a single body of what had been built up out of many members into one people, the Tri-Hypostatical Divinity took His own portion and preserved it unmingled for Himself. The remaining body, however, the part, which had been broken off from this portion and had inclined toward idolatry, the Tri-Hypostatical Divinity banished and drove out of Paradise, that is, out of the vineyard of His portion. Then, from that which was His part through faith according to election, which was itself taken from Adam's side, as it were taking for Himself a kind of little seed, the Theanthropos is Incarnate. This is to say that the second Adam is son of the first as born from his side without intercourse or emission of seed, and it is thus that the whole body of the first Adam and all his members are blessed. We mean that

❧

---

[206] Matthew 11:15

[207] Nicholas Cabasilas, *The Life in Christ*, Crestwood, St. Vladimir's Seminary Press, 1974, 43-44.

[208] Deuteronomy 6:4

the people of the Gentiles who had formerly been cast out are now, through Adam's son the Theanthropos, united by faith to the portion reserved from Adam's side. This is therefore what Paul says was known and predestined before the ages by the Tri-Hypostatical Divinity Who knows all things in advance, that all the nations from east to west are invited and, as many as believe, are joined to Him Who has become flesh from the side of their father, to the Theanthropos, the Son of God and son of Adam. So shall the two become One, as stated, "For He Himself is our peace, who has made both one, and has broken down the middle wall of separation;"[209] one body with the Theanthropos, His co-participants, brothers, and co-heirs with Him. Indeed, they become as the Theanthropos Himself, Who thus comprises the Nations, which had been turned out and scattered abroad. As many, though, as do not believe remain outside together with those who were removed from the portion of faith. Here the Jews were cast out and rejected because of their unbelief. For those who listen closely, this is also clear from the words of the Gospel all authority in the Heavenly Realm and on earth has been given to the Tri-Hypostatical Divinity. "And He said to them, 'Go into all the world and preach the gospel to every creature.'"[210] [211] An historical example is that of the Nation of Serbia. The Tri-Hypostatical Divinity through the Ecclesia has granted Theanthropic Nationhood to Serbia.[212]

The Heavenly Realm commences now, although it reaches complete fruition on the Day of the Lord. Some feel that that the Heavenly Realm is going to come after the general Resurrection, which is in some time and place far away. The answer is quite the contrary. The Tri-Hypostatical Divinity Who is the maker and creator of all things,

---

[209] Ephesians 2:14
[210] Mark 16:15-16
[211] Symeon, *Ethical*, Volume, 1, 94-95.
[212] Velimirovich, *Life*, 81, 92-100.

reigns forever over everything in the Heavenly Realm, and on earth, and beneath the earth. He also reigns over what has not yet come to be, since in Himself it exists already and because of whatever will happen through Him. No less does He reign over each one of us in justice and knowledge and truth.[213] As many therefore as are children of the light also become Sons of the Day, which is to come, and are, enabled to walk decently as in the day. The Day of the Lord will never come upon them, because they are already in it forever and continually. The Day of the Lord, in effect, is not going to be revealed suddenly to those who are illumined by the divine light, but for those who are in the darkness of the passions and spend their lives in the world hungering for the things of the world, for them it will be fearful and they will experience it as unbearable fire. However, this fire, which is the Tri-Hypostatical Divinity, will not appear in an entirely spiritual manner but, one might say, as bodiless embodied, in the same way as, according to the Evangelist, the Episcopates of old saw the Theanthropos after having risen from the dead. While He was being taken up into the Heavenly Realm, the Ethereal Beings said to them, "This *same* Jesus, who was taken up from you into heaven, will so come in like manner as you saw Him go into heaven."[214] Unless this is the case, how could the sinners, the unbelievers, the heretics and deniers of the Holy Spirit see Him, those who are blind and the eyes of whose nous are stopped-up by the mire of unbelief and sin?[215]

Since the Heavenly Realm has recommenced upon the Earth, it is obvious that Satan's realm is defeated and continues only in pretending to hold control of the Earth.

The outcome of the Heavenly Realm existing upon the Earth is

---

[213] Symeon, *Ethical*, Vol. 1, 137.
[214] Acts 1:11
[215] Symeon, *Ethical*, Vol. 1, 146-147.

that true peace is an expectation, as long as mankind is obedient to the Tri-Hypostatical Divinity.

The reality of how one has an understanding of a positive experience with the Tri-Hypostatical Divinity is confirmed. Be assured that the Theanthropos will say these things, and says them even now, to those who say they have the Holy Spirit in themselves, but He is covered over and hidden by the darkness of their passions and is not seen by the intelligible eyes of their nous. But to those who say that they know Him while admitting that they do not see the Light of His divinity, He says the following, "If you know Me, you would have known Me as light, for I am truly the light of the world."[216] Woe to any who asks, "When will the Day of the Lord come?" since they make no effort to understand. For the coming of the Lord has already taken place and is ever taking place in the Disciple and is at hand for all who desire it. He is the light of the world and said to His disciples that He would be with us until the consummation of the age. For those who are Disciple are not sons of darkness and of the night, that the Light should take us by surprise, but are Sons of the Light and of the Lord's Day. Therefore while we are yet alive we are in the Lord, and dying with Him we shall also live with Him.[217] We are both in the age to come and the day without evening, bridal chamber and bed, land of the meek and divine paradise, king and servant; just as He Himself has said, "Blessed *are* those servants whom the master, when he comes, will find watching. Assuredly, I say to you that he will gird himself and have them sit down *to eat,* and will come and serve them."[218] Therefore all these things, and others yet more, which it is not possible for a person to list, will the Theanthropos become for those who believe in Him. Nor will this be only in the age to come, but first in this life, then later in the future

---

[216] Refer to John 9:5
[217] Refer to Romans 14:8
[218] Luke 12:37

age as well. And if here more obscurely and there more perfectly, still the disciples do see plainly and receive here below, already, the first fruits of all that is beyond. For while the disciples do not receive all the promises here below, yet neither do they remain without any portion or taste of the things to come by hoping for everything there and merely existing here. Rather, since it is indeed through death that the Tri-Hypostatical Divinity arranges to give the disciples the Kingdom of the Resurrection, and incorruptibility and all of life everlasting, yet the disciples are already, without a doubt, become in soul partakers and communicants here below of the future good things, and are as it were incorruptible and immortal and Sons of the Tri-Hypostatical Divinity and Sons of Light and of the day, heirs of the Kingdom of the Heavenly Realm. The disciples clearly carry it around, because it is right here already through all perception and knowledge of their soul, unless the disciples are in some respect untried with respect to the faith or lacking in keeping the Divine Commandments. In the body, however, the disciples do not yet receive it. Just as the Theanthropos before His Resurrection, the disciples carry around a body as corruptible, and, encompassed and bound by it with respect to our nous, this cannot now accommodate receiving the entire glory, which has been revealed. In reflecting that ineffable ocean of glory, the disciples see a single drop of it, and for that reason say that for the moment we see as in a mirror and obscurely,[219] yet the disciples do see themselves spiritually as like Him Whom they see and Who sees them even in the present life. After the Resurrection, though, just as He Himself raised His own body from the tomb transformed by His Divine Power, so shall the disciples all receive bodies as spiritual, and, having first been likened to Him in our soul, shall then become like Him in both nous and body. This is to say that the disciple shall be like Him, human beings by nature and gods

---

[219] Refer to 1 Corinthians 13:12

by grace, just as He Himself is indeed the Tri-Hypostatical Divinity by nature Who in His goodness has taken the nature of man. "For we who are in *this* tent groan, being burdened, not because we want to be unclothed, but further clothed, that mortality may be swallowed up by life."[220] "For the earnest expectation of the creation eagerly waits for the revealing of the sons of God."[221] [222]

The Heavenly Realm is the abode of the Tri-Hypostatical Divinity.

There are many examples of sacrifices contained in *The Holy Bible*. There are types of sacrifices in the Old Covenant, which have relevance to the Heavenly Realm. The Theanthropos is the New Paschal Lamb. Concerning the Sacrifice itself there is a question that deserves to be considered. We are not concerned with a mere figurative sacrifice or symbolic shedding of blood, but with a true holocaust and sacrifice.

The disciples must ask themselves if the sacrifice is bread or the Body of the Theanthropos. Or, to put it in another way, are the offerings sacrificed before consecration or afterwards?

If it is bread, which is sacrificed, the disciple must ask how such a thing can be. Surely the Holy Mysteries do not consist in assisting at a sacrifice of bread, but rather that the Lamb of the Tri-Hypostatical Divinity, who by His death has taken away the sins of the world.

Yet it seems impossible that it can be the Theanthropos' Body, which is sacrificed. For this Body can no longer be slain or stricken, since now a stranger to the grave and to corruption, it has become immortal. Even if it were not impossible that it should suffer again, there would have to be executioners to perform the Crucifixion, and all those other elements, which were present at that, a Sacrifice in Truth. That is, if it were to be a true sacrifice, and not simply a representation.

How can this be, since the Theanthropos, being raised from the

---

[220] 2 Corinthians 5:4
[221] Romans 8:19
[222] Symeon, *Ethical*, Vol. 1, 163-5.

dead, can never die again? He has suffered once in time; He is offered once to bear the sins of many. Yet if He is sacrificed at every celebration of the Mysteries, He dies daily.

Is there an answer to these problems? Yes, the Sacrifice is accomplished neither before nor after the consecration of the bread, but at the very moment of the consecration itself. It is necessary thus to preserve all the Teachings of the Faith concerning Sacrifice, without overlooking any. What are these Teachings? In the first place, this Sacrifice is not a mere figure or symbol but a true sacrifice; secondly, that it is not the bread which is sacrificed, but the very Body of the Theanthropos; thirdly, that the Lamb of God is sacrificed once only, for all time. The essential act in the celebration of the Holy Mysteries is the transformation of the Divine Body and Blood; its aim is the sanctification of the Disciple, who through these Mysteries receive the Remission of sins and the inheritance of the Heavenly Realm. As a preparation for, and contribution to, this act and the purpose there are prayers, psalms, and readings from Holy Scripture; in short, all the sacred acts and forms which is said and done before and after the consecration of the elements. While it is true that the Tri-Hypostatical Divinity freely gives us all holy things and that the disciples bring him nothing, but they are absolute graces, He does nevertheless necessarily require that we should be fit to receive and preserve those who are not so disposed to being sanctified. It is in this way that He admits the disciple to the Mysteries of Baptism and Confirmation; in this way He receives the disciples at the divine banquet and allows us to participate at the solemn table.[223]

There is terminology found in *The Holy Bible* that clarifies the sacrifice of the Theanthropos, which is: atonement, forgiveness and

---

[223] Nicholas Cabasilas, *A Commentary On The Divine Liturgy*, London, S.P.C.K., 1983, 80, 81, 25

remission from guilt, and justice. Other terms of reference are expiation, justification, penalty, propitiation, reconciliation, redemption, ransom, satisfaction, vicarious and substitution.

Scientific Law relating to this topic comes from the time that the Ecclesia commenced on the Earth. The Ecclesia is an Eternal Organism.

Divine election is relating to the concept of the Tri-Hypostatical Divinity as His omnipresence, and the resulting omniscience. Divine election may be compared figuratively to a Byzantine Emperor taking in with a glance those who race and who wrestle in the arena, but does not thereby make himself responsible for the victory of the winners or the failures of the losers, the zeal, or in other cases the slackness, of the contestants being cause of their victory or defeat, understand with me that it is just so with the Tri-Hypostatical Divinity. When He endowed mankind with freewill, giving commandments to teach man instead of how man must oppose adversaries, He left it to the free choice of each either to oppose and vanquish the enemy, or to relax and be miserably defeated. Nor does He leave mankind entirely alone for He knows the weakness of human nature, but rather is present Himself with the Disciple and, indeed, allies Himself with those who choose to struggle, and mysteriously imbues the disciple with strength, and Himself accomplishes the victory over the adversary. An earthly emperor is unable to do so, since he is himself also a man, and is rather in need himself of assistance, just as any Believer requires.[224]

The Symbol of Faith of the Ecclesia clarifies for whom the Theanthropos died, "Who for us men and for our salvation came down from heaven and was incarnate of the Holy Spirit and the Virgin Mary, and became man."[225]

There are specific roles of the Tri-Hypostatical Divinity in relation

---

[224] Symeon, *Ethical*, Vol. 1, 86
[225] +Jonah, 64.

to Soteriology. The most effective data is contained within the area of the Ecclesia.

A case in point is the theory of eternal security. It is not the foreknowledge of the Tri-Hypostatical Divinity of those of the Disciple who, by their free choice and zeal, will prevail which is the cause of their victory, just as; again, it is not His knowing beforehand who will fall and be vanquished which is responsible for defeat. Instead, it is the zeal, deliberate choice, and courage of the Disciple, which brings about the victory. Faithfulness and sloth, irresolution and indolence, on the other hand comprise defeat and perdition. So, while reclining on the bed of worldly affection and love of pleasure, let us no one say "those whom the Tri-Hypostatical Divinity foreknew, them also He predestined," without perceiving just what it is one may be saying. He truly knows beforehand as inattentive and disobedient and lazy, but this is certainly not because He orders or foreordains it that one should have no power to repent, nor, if one wills it, to get up and obey. Anyone who says this is clearly calling the Tri-Hypostatical Divinity a liar. He says, "I have not come to call *the* righteous, but sinners, to repentance."[226] Many are lazy and unwilling to repent of evil, contradict Him, as it were, and call Him a liar Who never lies, when making such excuses as these. Why does mankind not believe instead with all one's nous that the Tri-Hypostatical Divinity has sent His Son upon the Earth for man's sake and salvation, which He knows, beforehand and predestined to become His brother and co-heir? Why should mankind not be eager to love Him with all their heart and to honour His saving commandments? Why does mankind not rather believe that, having been slaughtered for our sake, He will never abandon, nor allow anyone to perish? He says, "For God did not send His Son into the world to condemn the world,

---

[226] Luke 5:32

but that the world through Him might be saved."[227] Therefore, casting out of their nous all faithlessness, sloth, and hesitation, let us draw near with all our heart, with unhesitating faith and burning desire, which have been newly purchased with His precious blood. Indeed, with reverence for the price paid on our behalf, and with love for the Master Who pays, and having accepted His love for everyone, let us recognize that, if He has not wished to save by means of Himself us who have been purchased, He would not have come to earth, nor would He have been slain for mankind's sake. It is written, He has done this since He wills that all should be saved. Listen to Him say it Himself: "And if anyone hears My words and does not believe, I do not judge him; for I did not come to judge the world but to save the world."[228] The preceding argument has certainly established this clearly. The depth of knowledge of the Apostle's words and thoughts, so that all may learn that all who believe in the Theanthropos are foreknown, predestined, and become conformed to His image. All, as predestined, are called; and, as called, are also justified; and as justified, they are glorified. While those who perish who, after being baptized and believing in the Theanthropos, and becoming conformed to His image, do not keep themselves in this state, all who abide in it are saved.[229]

All people, especially ethicists, should see the reality of Soteriology clearly shown in *The Holy Bible*. Thus, it is disclosed that with respect to every sin or disposition, which is contrary to the Tri-Hypostatical Divinity, the Believer is directed to find deliverance from it by the Power of the indwelling Spirit, Who acts against Satan.[230] The Disciple thus seeks to live according to the Will of the Tri-Hypostatical Divinity.

The terms of Salvation are repentance; belief in the Theanthropos;

---

[227] John 3:17
[228] John 12:47
[229] Symeon, *Ethical*, Vol. 1, 87-89
[230] Chafer, III, 360

seeking out Ecclesia participating in Her Mysteries; constantly seeking the Will of the Tri-Hypostatical Divinity.

The Truth is presented through Soteriological research defining ethics. As stated above: "For this reason the Lives of the Saints are indeed experiential ethics that is applied ethics. The Lives of the Saints prove irrefutably that Ethics is nothing other than Applied Dogmatics."[231]

---

[231] Popovich, 46

Ecclesiology

Ecclesiology is the study of the Eternal Organism that exists in and through the Tri-Hypostatical Divinity. The Theanthropos is the Head of the Ecclesia. The Truth has great significance to the Ecclesia, since He is the only Head.

To understand the Ecclesia, it is imperative to be able to evaluate utilizing objective criteria. It does not make any sense at all to attempt to describe anything in negative terms, but this is especially true with reference to the Ecclesia.

The Ecclesia comes to Earth on the Day of Pentecost A.D. 33.[232] All of those ordained to the Episcopate, the Theotokos, and other Faithful in the Theanthropos, were all together in one room in Jerusalem. It was approximately nine o'clock in the morning. Suddenly a sound came from the Heavenly Realm, like the rush of a mighty wind, and it filled the entire house where they were sitting. Tongues that looked like fire descended on the Assembly and rested on each one of them. They were all filled with the Holy Spirit and began to speak in other languages, previously unknown to them. Thus the Holy Spirit, according to the promise of the Theanthropos, descended on the Faithful in the form of

---

[232] Technically the Ecclesia exists outside of time.

tongues of fire, as a sign that He gave the Faithful the ability and zeal to preach the Theanthropos' ethical teachings to all people. The Holy Spirit descends in the form of fire as a sign of the power to cleanse sins, to sanctify and warm the nous.[233]

The Ecclesia, as an Eternal Organism, is not historical but rather comes into history. One cannot rightly speak of the history of the Ecclesia, any more than one can technically speak of the Life of Jesus of Nazareth, since He is the Theanthropos.

The Theanthropos as Head of the Ecclesia has an Incarnation, with a pre-existence. The Theanthropos' Incarnation is His coming into time. With the crucifixion of the Theanthropos, He leaves time. The Theanthropos even though technically never leaving the Heavenly Realm, resumes His fully normal existence upon His crucifixion. The Theanthropos calls all mankind to return to their normal existence. The Ecclesia comes to the fallen creation – the Theanthropos being Her Head – both existing eternally.

The Ecclesia is Theanthropic, eternally Incarnated within the boundaries of time and space. She is here on Earth in this world, yet She is not of this world.[234] She is in the world to raise it on high where She Herself has Her origin. The Ecclesia is Ecumenical, Catholic, Theanthropic, and eternal. Consequently, it is blasphemous – an unpardonable blasphemy against the Tri-Hypostatical Divinity – to turn the Ecclesia into a national institution, to narrow Her down to petty, transient, time-bound aspirations and ways of doing things. Her purpose is to unite all mankind in the Theanthropos, without exception to nation, race, or social standing.[235]

This means that the Ecclesia grows through communities and when the Good News is accepted in a specific community becomes a

---

[233] Acts 2, and Slobodskoy, 381
[234] Refer to John 18:36
[235] Popovich, 23-24.

Theanthropic Community. When a Nation or Empire accepts the Good News, they become a Theanthropic Nation or Empire. The example of Holy Russia, which started as Rus AD 988.[236]

This procedure is comparable to the Old Covenant God gave to Israel as proven in the DVDs entitled, "The Israel Dilemma", and "Made in Israel".

Let us now look for proof of the Ecclesia being an Eternal Organism.

The Ecclesia's origin comes prior to time. The Ecclesia is Communion, or "gathering together," with the Tri-Hypostatical Divinity.

Prior to the creation of the physical existence, the spiritual existence comes into being. The Ethereal Beings are created who worship the Tri-Hypostatical Divinity. Consequently, Ethereal Beings are Members of the Ecclesia. This is confirmed through iconography that shows numerous Ethereal Beings, especially Michael and Gabriel who are Archangels.[237] The Prayer of the Entrance during the Divine Liturgy confirms Ethereal Beings' Membership in the Ecclesia, "O Master, Lord our God, who hast appointed in heaven orders and hosts of angels and archangels for the service of Thy glory: Grant that with our entrance there may be an entrance of holy angels, serving with us and glorifying Thy goodness. For unto Thee are due all glory, honor, and worship: to the Father and the Son and the Holy Spirit, now and ever and unto ages of ages. Amen."[238]

Prior to time, as we know it, Adam and Eve live in Communion with the Tri-Hypostatical Divinity. Consequently, Adam and Eve are Members of the Ecclesia, since they were in a state of illumination of the nous, this being the first degree of the vision of the Tri-Hypostatical

---

[236] John Strickland, *The Making of Holy Russia*. Jordanville, Holy Trinity Seminary Press, 2013,

[237] Monk, *These Truths We Hold*, South Canaan, St. Tikhon's Seminary Press, 1986, 24, 158, 161, 166, 173, 179, 188, 191, 194, 199, 201, 227, 277, 279, 281, 290 contain Ethereal Beings on icons.

[238] +Jonah, 40

Divinity. The Paradise that is tangible in a particular place and the Paradise that is intelligible are the Communion and union of man with the Tri-Hypostatical Divinity. The two Paradises interpenetrated since the Paradise of Eden receives the uncreated energy of the Tri-Hypostatical Divinity.[239]

The Ecclesia is an Eternal Organism, She comes to Earth in its time bound, Fallen situation. She offers mankind the opportunity to return to normal.

Proofs are provided from historical data.

The Ecclesia comes into time on the Day of Pentecost, A.D. 33 in the city of Jerusalem in the Province of Judaea. On the arrival of the Ecclesia three thousand come to join through the Mystery of Baptism.[240] The Ecclesia has no problem accommodating this. The structure is in place.

When a problem develops within the Ecclesiastical Community, those ordained to the Episcopate by the Theanthropos give immediate guidance to the Community. The Diaconate comes to resolve the problem.[241]

When it comes to resolving a major problem involving many Communities in the Ecclesia a Council is convened to settle this. "For it seemed good to the Holy Spirit, and to us"[242] is the phraseology utilized to describe the resolution. Decisions are as a result the Holy Spirit Who is one Hypostasis of the Tri-Hypostatical Divinity. This phraseology can only confirm the reality of the Ecclesia being an Eternal Organism. This phraseology continues to be utilized at Councils accepted by the Ecclesia, especially the Ecumenical Councils.

The rapid expansion and maturity of the Communities of the

---

[239] Hierotheos, *Mind*, 27.
[240] Refer to Acts 2:41
[241] Refer to Acts 6
[242] Acts 15:28

Ecclesia proves that She must be an Eternal Organism, since She does not proceed with support of the Roman Empire. Quite the contrary, She suffers persecution when She comes into time until She conquers the Roman Empire in the fourth century.

The Ecclesia conquers the Roman Empire through the Emperor Constantine the Great who moves the capital to New Rome, later called Constantinople. Historians refer to this as a new Empire, which they call the Byzantine Empire. This is really the Theanthropic Roman Empire.[243]

Within the first few centuries of this Empire, the theological research develops extensive works. However, is this due to a lack of understanding as many suppose? The conclusion of Basil the Great, in his treatise, *On The Holy Spirit*, is that all is understood by the Ecclesia, yet heretics wish to change some specifics. For instance, Basil states that the Temple should face east, and yet there is nothing in writing up to the time of his treatise to specify this reality.[244]

The dramatic heresy of the Pope of Rome is one of the saddest in the Ecclesia. In 1054, the Pope of Rome claimed the Head of the Ecclesia from the Theanthropos. The Ecclesia can have only one Head if She is an Eternal Organism.

Let us now consider the option of someone possibly being the Head of the Ecclesia, aside from the Theanthropos. Should the Ecclesia be an organization then the Popes of Rome may have some viability.

The reality is that if the Ecclesia is an organization, then the Head of the Ecclesia cannot be the Theanthropos. The Ascension takes place ten days prior to Pentecost. *The Holy Bible* clearly states that the Theanthropos is the Head of the Ecclesia.[245]

In Western Europe, the Ecclesiastical order gradually became

---

[243] Keen, 99-100 for reference to Theanthropic Nations
[244] Basil, 99.
[245] Refer to Ephesians 5:23

transformed into humanism. Since 1054 the Theanthropos has become more and more limited being confined to His humanity, eventually acknowledging an infallible man, the Pope of Rome. The Popes take everything away from the Theanthropos. A man takes the place of the Theanthropos as that which is of ultimate value and the measure of all, such as Truth. Western Christian humanistic maximalism, that is the infallible Pope, is fundamentally Protestantism since it removes the foundation of the Ecclesia from the eternal Theanthropos and attempts the placing of a finite man claiming to be the measure and criterion of all.[246]

Jesus of Nazareth is the Eternal Head of the Ecclesia, since He is Theanthropos and He is the Second Hypostasis of the Tri-Hypostatical Divinity.

Jesus of Nazareth ordains people. Let us see what *The Holy Bible* states. "And he ordained twelve, that they should be with him, and that he might send them forth to preach, And to have power to heal sicknesses, and to cast out devils: And Simon he surnamed Peter; And James the son of Zebedee, and John the brother of James; and he surnamed them Boanerges, which is, The sons of thunder: And Andrew, and Philip, and Bartholomew, and Matthew, and Thomas, and James the son of Alphaeus, and Thaddaeus, and Simon the Canaanite, And Judas Iscariot, which also betrayed him: and they went into an house."[247] "You did not choose Me, but I chose you and appointed you that you should go and bear fruit, and *that* your fruit should remain, that whatever you ask the Father in My name He may give you. These things I command you, that you love one another."[248] It would appear that Jesus of Nazareth must be the Head of the Ecclesia, since He ordains to the Episcopate. Those who hold the Episcopate may ordain to Presbyter

---

[246] Popovich, 89-90.
[247] Mark 3:14-19 (A.V.)
[248] John 15: 16-17

or the diaconate but may not ordain another to the Episcopate. *The Rudder* requires one to be ordained to the Episcopate by two or three holding the Episcopate.[249]

A new liturgical year takes place in the new Pascha. Pascha is the celebration of the Resurrection, fifty days prior to Pentecost. This is the New Covenant mentioned in Jeremiah's prophecy,[250] and confirmed in the Book of Hebrews.[251] The formula utilized by the Theanthropos through the Apostolic Canons confirms the Ecclesia.[252] All others, who claim to be Christians, celebrate on the wrong date, thus confirming their heretical views.

Jesus of Nazareth, the Theanthropos, is Head of the Ecclesia Who communicates from the Heavenly Realm. *The Holy Bible* confirms this fact, "to Jesus the Mediator of the new covenant, and to the blood of sprinkling that speaks better things than *that of* Abel.

See that you do not refuse Him who speaks. For if they did not escape who refused Him who spoke on earth, much more *shall we not escape* if we turn away from Him who *speaks* from heaven, whose voice then shook the earth; but now He has promised, saying, *'Yet once more I shake not only the earth, but also heaven.'"*[253]

The Theanthropos communicates to the Ecclesia through His Ecclesiastical Communities. The methodology of this communication is described in *Revelation* chapter 1. In this example, the Theanthropos communicates to His Communities in the Roman Province of Asia through John the President of the Synod of Asia. These Communities, in turn passed this Revelation onto the Ecclesia in Her entirety. The Ecclesia always confirms Her communications from Her Head.

---

[249] Nicodemus, Apostolic Canon 1, 1-4
[250] Refer to Jeremiah 31:31-32
[251] Chapter 12
[252] Nicodemus, Apostolic Canon 7, 9-20
[253] Hebrews 12:24-26

Communications from the Theanthropos, in His capacity as Head of the Ecclesia continues to this day.

The Theanthropos communicates from the Heavenly Realm to His Ecclesia. Is it reasonable to expect that with thethropos communicating from the Heavenly Realm, He is somehow not including the Ecclesia present in the Heavenly Realm?

The Ecclesia present in the Heavenly Realm has far better understanding of Who She is outside of time than does the Ecclesia enslaved by time. The Theanthropos has His presence in the Heavenly Realm until the Heavenly Realm comes to Earth at the end of time.[254]

The Ecclesiastical Community is One through the Theanthropos. Every aspect of the Ecclesiastical Community, Her Temple, organization, structure, administration, finances, and property must be Theanthropic. She is Catholic; that is full, complete, and whole with the Theanthropos dwelling as His Body in fullness of life, Grace and Truth. She is Apostolic since She is founded upon Apostolic doctrine and Tradition. She must understand Herself as an Apostolic Community with a missionary purpose. She consists of Disciples who are prophets as a holder of the Royal Priesthood.[255]

The Reformation introduced an innovation of how the Holy Spirit gave direction to the Ecclesia. Generally, the Reformation maintained the individual approach. The Tri-Hypostatical Divinity manifests Himself through individual people. The aspect of Community is discounted as everyone is entitled to participate in a plurality of denominations. *The Holy Bible* refutes plurality: "*There is* one body and one Spirit, just as you were called in one hope of your calling; one Lord, one faith, one

---

[254] Refer to Revelation 21
[255] Thomas Hopko, *Speaking the Truth in Love*, Crestwood, St. Vladimir's Seminary Press, 2004, 85-89

baptism; one God and Father of all, who *is* above all, and through all, and in you all."[256]

The Reformation promotes the concept of individual interpretation of *The Holy Bible*. Theoretically, this is dependent upon knowledgeable the Faithful who have theological expertise. Instead, Scripture states: "And so we have the prophetic word confirmed, which you do well to heed as a light that shines in a dark place, until the day dawns and the morning star rises in your hearts; knowing this first, that no prophecy of Scripture is of any private interpretation, for prophecy never came by the will of man, but holy men of God spoke *as they were* moved by the Holy Spirit."[257]

Martin Luther made the unbelievable decision to reject certain *Books* of *The Holy Bible* that had been confirmed by the Mind of the Ecclesia. Martin Luther's radical recommendation was the rejection of the first and second Epistles of *John*, *James*, and the Book of *Revelation*. In addition, he rejected specific Books of the Old Testament, which were found in the Ecclesia's official text, known as the Septuagint. These Books are now known as the Apocrypha.[258]

Even the eminent theological scholars of the Reformation fail to understand what specific Scripture means. John Calvin fails to write a Commentary on *the Book of Revelation*, since he is unable to understand this Letter to the Ecclesia. Yet this Book is one of the few Scripture, which should be understood. Let us see what this Book says, "Blessed *is* he who reads and those who hear the words of this prophecy, and keep those things which are written in it; for the time *is* near."[259]

As Western European Empires expanded throughout the globe there was an era regarded as one of "Missions." The perception is that

---

[256] Ephesians 4:4-6
[257] 2 Peter 1:19-22
[258] Frank Schaeffer, *Dancing Alone*, Brookline, Holy Cross Orthodox Press, 1994, 76
[259] Revelation 1:3

the Gospel Message was expanded throughout the world by highly organized groups of missionaries who brought civilization to ignorant peoples. Unfortunately, many Christian countries interpreted the situation, in light of some Scripture that indicated that genocide was appropriate. Entire nations of native peoples in North America were exterminated, whether these people became Christian or not.

During this era, the Ecclesia also utilized missions to share the Gospel Message. The methodology of missions in the Ecclesia has followed a specific pattern. A small number of those called to the Episcopate would migrate to specific territories to share – both training and learning from the indigenous population. For the most part, this was accomplished by the fact that indigenous people had no written language. The one bearing the Episcopate would then set-up training for those called to various Holy Orders, so that the Community could develop. This new Ecclesiological Community perfects the natural community with due recognition for those whom the Tri-Hypostatical Divinity had called to governmental responsibilities. Often the leadership of communities would be more interested in learning than others in these communities. This is natural since they would wish the best for their communities. The success of the Ecclesiastical missions was quite dramatic.

An example of the dramatic difference between missions of Christian countries and the Ecclesia can be appreciated by observing the first martyrs in North America.

The first Christian missionary martyred in North America was Jean de Brébeuf who was a member of the Society of Jesus. His mission was to the Huron nation. Warriors of the Six Nations killed him, since his country, France, was assisting the Huron nation against the Six Nations.

The first Ecclesiastical martyr in North America is Peter the Aleut, who was captured by Spanish soldiers near San Francisco. Roman

Catholic Priests martyr him, claiming that he was a schismatic or a heretic. The Aleutians are a Community within the Ecclesia.

The results of these great Christian missionary endeavours are quite poor. India, where the Gospel Message comes as a result of Thomas ordained by the Theanthropos, does not return to Christianity for example. The results of the Ecclesiastical missions still bear fruit with the numerous Communities living the Gospel Message. Missions start with the Ecclesia coming to time, and She continuously has missions.

In the twentieth century the first aspects of what is commonly referred to as the Charismatic phenomenon occurred. This reinforces the individualistic concept of Soteriology and the relationship with the Tri-Hypostatical Divinity. The Charismatic phenomenon is pertinent due to the reality of its affect on all Christian groups. Unlike other movements within the Christian developments the Charismatic phenomenon has participants in numerous Reformation denominations, and the Roman papacy. This is rather unique in the annals of Christian history. This is a harking back by many to the Day of Pentecost A.D. 33. One cannot truly relive history.

The Charismatic phenomenon is actually an attempt by individuals to have a new Pentecost. The problem with this is a lack of realization that Pentecost is the coming of the Ecclesia into time. The Ecclesia is a plurality of phenomena rather that an individual phenomenon. Charismatic is a synonym for Mystery in the Ecclesia.

All of this confirms that these aspects are beyond time constraints. The various historical aspects pale when compared with the active vitality of the Ecclesia that does not depend upon the strength of Her Communities in time but is resilient as a result of the Heavenly Realm where the Ecclesia exists in perfection.

The historical aspects of the Ecclesia are pertinent only if taken into account with the timeless reality of the Ecclesia. God the Holy Spirit directs the Ecclesia confirming Her in Truth, as stated in the Symbol of Faith. He is not time-bound; however, He is the Tri-Hypostatical Divinity. This can never be forgotten.

The Holy Spirit exists outside of time constraints, so the Ecclesia must also exist outside of time constraints. It may be argued that the Ecclesia is an organization, yet this is not a technically correct term. The organization of the Ecclesia is comparable to the organization of any organism. This does not negate the reality of the Ecclesia being an Eternal Organism. Quite the contrary, the style of organization is more akin to timelessness than one of time constraints.

Those who are called to Holy Orders may have a title of a Community that may not exist in time, yet this does not change the viability of the Call. For instance, Antioch no longer exists in the Roman Province of Syria. There is one who holds the Episcopate of Antioch recognized by the Mother Ecclesia of Jerusalem. If the Ecclesia is only an organization there could never be an Ecclesiastical Community in an apparently non-existent community. Communities in danger are permitted to remove Her Faithful in order to continue the Ecclesiastical Community. The Mother Ecclesia of Jerusalem has done this. The Theanthropos gives direction to the Ecclesia to remove Herself in times of danger. He says, "But woe to those who are pregnant and to those who are nursing babies in those days! And pray that your flight may not be in winter or on the Sabbath."[260]

Ecclesiastical Communities consequently may not exist in time, since She no longer has a continuous Community. How can this be if She is simply an organization in time? Time constrained organizations flair in and out of existence. When studying the history of a country, one must remember that a country may have numerous names and configurations. There is nothing as continuous as the Ecclesia. For

---

[260] Matthew 24:19-20

instance, the country known as the United Kingdom is an erratic group of numerous peoples who invaded and stayed. The United Kingdom has been known or made up of the following: Briton, Celtic lands, the Roman Province of Briton, Essex, Wales, Ireland, England, Scotland, Great Britain, and Gaul.

Should the Ecclesia be thought of only in Her historical setting and what would this mean? The answer will prove disastrous if She is considered Earthbound in time.

Errors can be easily determined if the Ecclesia is assessed as an Eternal Organism. Historical facts only confirm the nature of the Ecclesia as an Eternal Organism.

One short formula for ascertaining the Unity of the Ecclesia is the timeless consecration of the Holy Altar in the Temple at the inauguration. There are three aspects in one, a tri-unity, which constitutes the Ecclesiastical Ethos of the Community. One is the Holy Altar; the second is the consecrator – the one called to the Episcopate, and the third is the Saint's relics. The Holy Altar is dedicated by the one called to the Episcopate, who places the Saint's relics under the Holy Altar. This shows that the Holy Altar, the one called to the Episcopate, and the Saints form the axis of the unity of the Ecclesia, as well as the spiritual life of the Community. The Holy Altar cannot be understood without the one called to the Episcopate and the Saints. The one called to the Episcopate cannot be understood apart from the Holy Altar and the Divine Liturgy, the centre of Mysteries, nor can Saints be understood apart from the Holy Altar and the one called to the Episcopate. A disturbance of these three centres of Ecclesiastical life does not constitute the Ethos and Mind of the Ecclesia.

The Ecclesia proves Her Truth since She supports the three unifying centres of spiritual life. Heretics have scattered the unity of the Ecclesia since some disregard the Saints, others undervalue the Holy Altar, and, in general the sacramental life of the Ecclesia.[261]

The twenty-first century provides freedom for many of the Ecclesiastical Communities. There is a tremendous requirement to accept theanthropic education and to apply it completely for every educational institution – primary, secondary, tertiary, from the greatest to smallest. Theanthropic education radiates, illuminates, enlightens with the only inextinguishable and true Light for the entire Earth, namely Jesus of Nazareth, the Theanthropos. Darkness cannot extinguish or hide this Light, not even the darkness of the West. Only this is capable of expelling all darkness from man, from society, from people, and from the state. This, the only true Light, illuminates every person into the nucleus of his /her being and reveals to each one of us our own immorality, our own divine and eternal brother. It teaches us that only then can mankind, societal, people and national problems be understood and solved when they are examined through the Theanthropos.

The main guidelines and characteristics of Theanthropic Education can be formulated as follows:

1. Mankind is a being who can be perfected and completed in the most ideal and real way by the Theanthropos and in the Theanthropos.
2. The perfection of mankind by the Theanthropos takes place with the help of the evangelical witnesses.
3. The illuminated and educated of mankind sees in every person his immortal and eternal relative.
4. Every human work and action – philosophy, science, geography, art, education, culture, manual labour, etc. – receives eternal

---

[261] Hierotheos, *Mind*, 82-84.

value when sanctified and receives meaning from the Theanthropos.

5. True enlightenment and education is accomplished through holy living according to the Gospel Message.

6. The Saints are the most perfect illuminators and educators; the more holy a person is the better educator and illuminator he/she becomes.

7. School is the second half of the heart of the Theanthropos – the first being the Ecclesia.

8. At the centre of all centres and of all ideas and labours stand the Theanthropos and His theanthropic society, the Ecclesia.[262]

Theanthropic education is the eternal Quest of the Ecclesia, reaching beyond time.

The Ecclesia exists on Earth after time has been extinguished.

Every time a development comes to the Ecclesia, She is prepared since She exists outside of time.

The Ecclesia is acknowledged as an Eternal Organism. Since all organisms are organized, it follows that the Ecclesia is organized as well.

For the Ecclesia to exist upon the planet Earth and be an Eternal Organism requires a theanthropic personage to bridge the gap. As seen in research under Christology this is found in the historical person known as Jesus of Nazareth, acknowledged as the Theanthropos.

The basic scientific Laws relating to the Ecclesia are contained in the book entitled, *The Rudder*.[263] The Theanthropos ordains seventy to the Episcopate, to whom He teaches the concepts and precepts of the Ecclesia.[264] As questions arose relating to the Ecclesia, Theanthropic Emperors convene Ecumenical Councils. Ecumenical Councils consist

---

[262] Popovich, 63-64.

[263] Nicodemus, xxxviii-xxxix

[264] Ibid., xxvii

of all who hold the Episcopate in the Ecclesia. The decisions of all Ecumenical Councils start with the declaration, "For it seemed good to the Holy Spirit, and to us…"[265] These decisions are confirmed by the entire Ecclesia. All Ecumenical decisions are included in *The Rudder*.

One of the first written documents of the Ecclesia is the Word of the Tri-Hypostatical Divinity to mankind. The books contained in Scripture are found in Canon 85 of the Apostolic Canons. *The Rudder* now contains a revised list.[266]

The Rudder explains the significance of the Mother Ecclesia in Jerusalem. The Theanthropos trained and declared who the first person was to receive the Episcopate of the Mother Ecclesia of Jerusalem. The present holder of the Episcopate of the Mother Ecclesia of Jerusalem is confirmed by the reception of the Holy Light on Pascha, the first day of the Ecclesiastical year. The Holy Light confirms the correct date for Pascha, as well as the correct holder of the Episcopate.[267]

There may be many claimants to the Episcopate of the Mother Ecclesia, but only one receives the recognition of the Holy Light. There are many claimants who claim prerogative of "first" among those of the Episcopate, but there is only one Mother Ecclesia. Every National Ecclesia has Her source in the Mother Ecclesia. This is an historical fact.

These facts clearly establish that the Ecclesia is a visible Eternal Organism existing on Earth. With reference to Nations, *The Rudder* clarifies that the Ecclesia grants this right through the confirming the Autocephaly to Cyprus in Canon 8 of the Third Ecumenical Council. Autocephaly is granted by Letters Patent such as the one issued by the Episcopate of Constantinople with reference to the granting

---

[265] Acts 15:28
[266] Nicodemus, Canon 32, 623-624
[267] This historical fact is confirmed by Slobodskoy, 453 - 456, as well as on the Internet including: http://www.holyfire.org/eng .

of Autocephaly to Serbia in 1219.[268] As a result of this document, Stefan the Zupan was anointed as King of Serbia.[269] The Ecclesia confers Nationhood through the granting of Autocephaly. The usual methodology of attaining Autocephalous status is simply by the Ecclesia in a nation becoming a Theanthropic Nation, such Ireland after the ministry of St. Patrick uniting the various tribes into one Theanthropic Nation of Ireland. The confirmation of the Autocephalous statis of Ireland in the motto "Erin Go Bragh".[270]

There are some theologians who differentiate between Israel and the Ecclesia. Israel is a term to denote a Nation Who has a relationship (i.e., autocephaly) with the Tri-Hypostatical Divinity. The difference between a country and a Nation is described in *Holy Russia Inside The Soviet Union*.[271] The relationship between the Nation and the Ecclesia are clearly enumerated in *The Patriarch and the Prince*.[272] The two books utilize the scientific Laws found in *The Rudder* to clarify the practicality of these Laws. The relationship between the Ecclesia and the Nation (including an Empire) is best described as a Symphony.

The order of the Ecclesia is clearly understood. The Theanthropos instructed those with the Episcopate, ordaining them to the office of Apostle,[273] and introducing the Ecclesia to mankind. These instructions are contained in the 85 Canons of the Apostles. For example, Canon 1 states: "A Bishop must be ordained by two or three other Bishops."[274]

---

[268] Velimirovich, *Life*, 81
[269] Ibid, Chapter 29
[270] Erin Go Bragh Pronunciation https://www.youtube.com/watch?v=NoTQuwO3Z0o
[271] Mitrofan clearly explains why the Theanthropic Nation of Russia continues to exist even while the country is called the Soviet Union. This book was written prior to the fall of the Soviet Union.
[272] Photios of Constantinople, *The Patriarch and the Prince*, Brookline, Holy Cross Orthodox Press, 1982. Photios of Constantinople wrote this treatise to Michael the first Ruler of Bulgaria
[273] Refer to John 15:15-17
[274] Nicodemus, 1

The Mission of the Ecclesia is to make every one of Her Faithful, organically and in person, one with the Person of the Theanthropos; to turn their sense of self into a sense of the Theanthropos, and their self-knowledge (self-awareness) into Theanthropos-knowledge (Theanthropos-awareness); for their life to become the life in Theanthropos and for the Theanthropos; their personality to become personality in Theanthropos and for the Theanthropos; that within them might live not they themselves but the Theanthropos in them.[275] This is confirmed in *The Holy Bible*, "I have been crucified with Christ; it is no longer I who live, but Christ lives in me; and the *life* which I now live in the flesh I live by faith in the Son of God, who loved me and gave Himself for me."[276]

To some theologians, there are only two "ordinances" in the Ecclesia, those being, "ritual baptism and the Lord's Supper."[277] There is no consideration for Holy Orders, and Matrimony, for instance. Holy Orders and Matrimony are extremely important Mysteries in the Ecclesia. Holy Orders are important enough to be placed in Apostolic Canon 1. Errors relating to the Ecclesia arrive as a result of attempting to disengage Mysteries in the Ecclesia.

Some theologians claim that there are only seven "Sacraments". These seven Sacraments are sometimes understood as Mysteries, the term "Sacrament" coming from the Latin and "Mystery" coming from the Greek. The more precise term is "Mystery".[278]

There is little doubt that there are seven major Mysteries within the Ecclesia. These seven Mysteries are: 1) Baptism, 2) Chrismation, 3) Eucharist, 4) Repentance, 5) Holy Orders, 6) Matrimony, and 7) Unction. There are more Mysteries, since a Mystery is composed of

---

[275] Popovich, 23
[276] Galatians 2:20
[277] Chafer, IV, 151
[278] For a clear explanation refer to Pomazansky, 261.

the natural (i.e., the material and visible) and the supernatural (i.e., the spiritual and invisible).[279]

The Ecclesia comes to the Earth on the Day of Pentecost A.D. 33. There are four reasons, namely: 1) the Ecclesia requires purification through the Blood of the Theanthropos; 2) the Resurrection is required; 3) the Ascension is required; and 4) the Advent of the Holy Spirit is required.[280]

The Ecclesia is an Eternal Organism. Research confirms that the Ecclesia is an Eternal Organism: only in the Theanthropos is there salvation; the Ecclesia is not a human organization, but a Theanthropic Organism; and the Ecclesia is the Body of the Theanthropos, He being the Head and the Faithful being His Body. With the Advent of the Theanthropos, the Ecclesia commences on Earth in perpetuity.[281]

The Ecclesia produces *The Holy Bible* as confirmed in Scripture, "knowing this first, that no prophecy of Scripture is of any private interpretation, for prophecy never came by the will of man, but holy men of God spoke *as they were* moved by the Holy Spirit."[282]

The Temple of the Ecclesia is extremely significant. The interior of a Temple is usually a domed octagon following the prototype of the Great Temple of Holy Wisdom built by the Theanthropic Roman Emperor Justinian. The architecture can denote a true Temple of the Ecclesia since eight, according to numerology, symbolizes the Resurrection[283] and the sign of the Age to come.[284] One can immediately sense the

---

[279] Frangopoulos, 204

[280] Chafer, IV, 45

[281] Professor John Karmiris, cited by Hierotheos, *Mind*, 24-35

[282] 2 Peter 1:20, 21

[283] The Resurrection occurs on the eighth day, Sunday.

[284] The New Heavenly Realm and Earth already present in the Ecclesia

Temple of the Tri-Hypostatical Divinity as soon as one enters the building.[285]

The Temple in Moscow Resurrected - Originally in honour of the War of 1812 – communists destroyed – built to celebrate the Bimillennial in AD 2000

The Truth leads the Ecclesia, since She is the purveyor of Truth.

The Theanthropos is the only Head of the Ecclesia, and She in turn grants Theanthropic status on Nations and Empires. As a result, the ethos of communities is relevant in respect to a starting point when determining the ethics in seeking the Truth.

[285] Peter Jeffreys, *Saint George's Greek Orthodox Church An Architectural and Iconographic Guide*, Toronto, University of Toronto Press Inc., 2000.

New Data:

The Ecclesia is responsible for training catechumens. There are now exceptional books to train catechumens in the Faith. There is Anne Fields book, *From Darkness to Light* which takes the training which was utilized in the early years of the Ecclesia returning to the Earth, AD 33 onward, a newer excellent book for catechumens is written by Micharl Keiser's book, *Spread the Word*, which is contemporary.

Canadian Orthodox are utilizing DVDs primarily excellent for training catechumens to become disciples of Christ in forensic faith based on books by J. Warner Wallace.

Catechumens training: *Person of Interest* and *The Truth in True Crime* – based on his books.

Discipleship training: *Cold Case Christianity* and *Forensic Faith* – based on his books.

Orthodox Spiritualty Series are exceptional examples for discipleship training!

Resiliency in the Ecclesia has been proven from the Pskov Caves Monastery, which survived throughout the times of persecution in the Union of Soviet Socialist Republics (USSR). The data supplied is inspiring for all who are facing persecution.[286]

---

[286] Archimandrite Tikhon Shevkunov, Everyday Saints and Other Stories. Dallas, Pokrov Publications, 2012.

CHAPTER

9

Pneumatology

Pneumatology is the study of one Hypostasis of the Tri-Hypostatical Divinity, namely the Holy Spirit. This is the methodology through which the Tri-Hypostatical Divinity communicates the Truth Who is the Theanthropos.

There are numerous theories relating to The Holy Spirit, but most are not measured against Laws recognized by the Ecclesia in the Symbol of Faith. The relationship between the Holy Spirit and the Ecclesia is clearly delineated in the Symbol of Faith. We shall start from this point.

The Symbol of Faith states: "And in the Holy Spirit, the Lord, the Giver of Life, who proceeds from the Father; who with the Father and the Son is worshipped and glorified; who spoke by the prophets. In one, Holy, Catholic, and Apostolic Church. I acknowledge one baptism for the remission of sins. I look for the resurrection of the dead and the life of the world to come. Amen."[287]

The Ecclesia declares that the Holy Spirit is one Hypostasis in the Tri-Hypostatical Divinity, as every atom on earth also represents a

---

[287] +Jonah, 61.

tri-unity. The Holy Spirit is called the Giver of Life because He bestows life, restores life, brings to life, and resurrects.[288]

There is some dispute in the next declaration of the Ecclesia with reference to the Procession. The first innovation, or heresy, was the addition to the eighth article of the Symbol of Faith with the Latin word "*filioque*," meaning "and from the Son," and signifying that the Holy Spirit proceeds from the Father and from the Son, contrary to the words of our Lord, who said: "But when the Helper comes, whom I shall send to you from the Father, the Spirit of truth who proceeds from the Father, He will testify of Me."[289] The addition of "and from the Son" bisects the hypostasis of the Holy Spirit cutting it in two, so to speak, and makes the Son a father, an allegation which is nothing short of blasphemous and heretical.

The Second Ecumenical Council, which supersedes the Symbol of Faith of the First Ecumenical Council, defines that no one has the right to add anything to or to subtract anything from the Symbol of Faith as established by the Universal Ecclesia. The minutes of both of these Councils were attested to and signed by all of the participants, including the representatives of the Episcopates of the Ecclesiastical Community of Rome then holding office. The addition of "*filioque*" is a blasphemy against the Holy Spirit, and the source of it is Satan and according to the words of the Theanthropos, "Therefore I say to you, every sin and blasphemy will be forgiven men, but the blasphemy *against* the Spirit will not be forgiven men."[290] "Proceeds" signifies the manner of generation, and not the act of sending or the act of being sent. The Son is begotten only by the Father, or, as is more to the point and closer to the meaning of the Greek word in question, is yielded only

[288] Nikolai Velimirovich, *The Faith of Chosen People*, Grayslake, The Free Serbian Orthodox Diocese, 1988, 63-64
[289] John 15:26
[290] Matthew 12:31

by the Father; two branches from the same root, brothers, as it were; effects of the causeless, initial, and absolute cause; timeless, eternal, inalterable, everlasting, because their being is derived hypostatically from the timeless, eternal, inalterable and everlasting Father; being simultaneously, and not alternating, at the same time the Father, at the same time the Son, and together and at the same time the Mind, Speech, and Spirit – or, *Nous*, *Logos*, and *Pneuma*; the first Mind (Father) begets (generates) the Speech or Word (*Logos*) and yields (prolates) the Spirit to the Logos and the Son, and through Him to the Ecclesia. That is why the Theanthropos says, "whom the Father will send in My name."[291] Jesus of Nazareth, as victor, legally acquired the right to send the Holy Spirit to the Ecclesia, and the Father sends the Holy Spirit in His name.[292]

In the Ecclesia the past is contemporary and that which is present remains so on account of the living past, since the Theanthropos who is "the same yesterday, today, and forever"[293] continuously lives in His Theanthropic Body by means of the same Truth, the same holiness, the same goodness, the same life and establishes the past in the present. Thus, to a living Theanthropic Ethical understanding and conscience, all members of the Ecclesia, from the Episcopates called to the Apostolic Office to those who have recently fallen asleep, are contemporary since they continuously live in the Heavenly Realm. Further, today in every true Theanthropic individual one can find all of the Holy Episcopates, Martyrs, and Holy Fathers. For the Ecclesia these are more real than many of their contemporaries. This sense of the catholic unity of faith, life, and knowledge constitutes the essence of the Ecclesial reality. It is this understanding that reveals the Truth of the Theanthropos' unceasing, life-giving power which is revealed unremittingly in the

[291] John 14:26
[292] Nicodemus, 204-206
[293] Hebrews 13:8

119

theanthropic life of the Ecclesia by the unity, holiness, catholicity, and apostolicity of the Ecclesia's faith, life, and Truth. For to profess to be disciples of Theanthropos means this: to be part of the continuous struggle that leads from man to the Theanthropos, that is, to be involved in the unending improvement of oneself through the Theanthropic Mysteries, struggles, and virtues. Here the disciples of the Theanthropos are never alone. Every feeling, act, and thought is individual and universal, not merely personal and catholic but theanthropic. When a disciple of the Theanthropos ponders something, he knows that the choir of Ethereal Beings and the entire Ecclesia participates mystically with him in his struggle. The disciples of the Theanthropos do not belong only to himself, but to all the Saints and, through them, to the Theanthropos. When he examines his own nous, the disciple of the Theanthropos reflects: my nous is nothing unless it is filled and perfected by the Holy Spirit. In the life and nous of an disciple of the Theanthropos nothing takes place according to a human desire or will, but everything occurs according to the Theanthropos. Through the exercise of evangelical virtues, the disciples of the Theanthropos concentrates on the Tri-Hypostatical Divinity: his nous, soul and will concentrate through the aid of the Holy Spirit. Whatever belongs to him is gathered and universalized in the Theanthropos. With his entire being, he understands that the Ecclesia is always holy and catholic and that the Theanthropic attribute is the unaltered characteristic of the Ecclesia. The Theanthropic person maintains a continuous sense of theanthropic catholicity, which preserves and kindles through prayer and humility. They never preach about themselves; they never boast; they never remain entirely within their base human nature; they never idealize humanism. The Episcopates in Council once and for all gave the definition of the Ecclesial dimension of divine humanity: "For it seemed good to the Holy Spirit".[294] First, the Holy Spirit, and then, us, the "us" in as much as one allows the Holy Spirit to act through each one of us.[295]

The Mystery of Baptism is the means of complete purification. This Mystery represents the doors through which people enter the Ecclesia. They do not enter two or three times, but once. Consequently, there is only one baptism. The Mystery of Baptism, with the Mystery of Chrismation, continues to the present day. The Theanthropos commands "Go therefore and make disciples of all the nations, baptizing them in the name of the Father and of the Son and of the Holy Spirit".[296] This is the healing and soteriological-bearing commandment carried out to the letter, and which the Ecclesia continues to carry out up to the present day.[297]

The Resurrection comes at the end of time. Then countless billions of persons shall be clothed in light, imperishable clothing, in heavenly bodies similar to that of the Theanthropos.[298]

The Life of the Age to come is commonly referred to as the Second Advent of the Theanthropos. This is the Paradise for which all of mankind has longed. Paradise is one of the sweetest names of that kingdom. Paradise is our true homeland.[299]

The role of the Holy Spirit is in conjunction with the Ecclesia. The Theanthropos is the Head of the Ecclesia, yet the Holy Spirit has relevance to the entire Ecclesia.

The reality of the deity of the Holy Spirit is delineated in Chapter 1 through the attributes of the Tri-Hypostatical Divinity.

There are types and symbols of the Holy Spirit, namely: oil, water,

---

[294] Acts 15:28
[295] Popovich, 85-87
[296] Matthew. 28:19
[297] Velimirovich, *Faith*, 78
[298] Ibid, 85
[299] Ibid, 97

fire, wind, dove, and seal. There is much research relating to the realities of these. Mysteries are a cooperative function between man and the Tri-Hypostatical Divinity, often in the Hypostasis of the Holy Spirit.

Oil is utilized in the Mystery of Chrismation. The Mystery of Chrismation is performed usually immediately after the Mystery of Baptism, comprising together with it a single rite in the Ecclesia. The performer of the Mystery, usually a Presbyter, anoints with Holy Chrism making the Sign of the Cross on the: brow, breast, both hands, both feet, and between the shoulders. He says each time, "the seal of the gift of the Holy Spirit."[300] This Mystery is also performed on those who are uniting to the Ecclesia from heretical communities as one of the means of being united to the Ecclesia. It is the culminating act of being united to the Ecclesia, the confirmation or seal of union, and the seal of the grace-given powers, which are bestowed in it for strengthening and growth in spiritual life.[301]

Water is observed in the Mystery of Holy Baptism. Through this Mystery one receives the first fruits of the Holy Spirit and rebirth comes for the Faithful with the beginning of another life, and a seal, phylactery and illumination.[302]

The Mystery of Baptism takes place in a Mikveh, which is still performed in Judaism.[303] https://www.youtube.com/watch?v=ofnBSNGWdfY.

Fire is observed in the Mother Ecclesiastical Community of Jerusalem confirming the correct date for Pascha, as well as the correct person holding the Episcopate of the Ecclesiastical Community of Jerusalem. Candles in bundles of thirty-three are lighted, yet the flame

---

[300] Philip, 159
[301] Pomazansky, 270
[302] John of Damascus cited by Frangopoulos, 209
[303] Mikveh: https://www.youtube.com/watch?v=ofnBSNGWdfY

does not burn the people who are in the Temple during the service. This was discussed with proofs under Ecclesiology.

Wind is alluded to at the commencement of the Ecclesia coming to Earth on Pentecost A.D. 33. This is described in Acts 2:2. the literal translation is "Like as of a violent wind borne along."[304] Observe how the Scripture states, "like as," and rightly, that one may not have gross sensible notions of the Spirit. It says "as of a violent wind" which betokens the exceeding vehemence of the Spirit, but it was not a wind.[305]

The Dove is a manifestation related to the Baptism of Jesus of Nazareth. "When He had been baptized, Jesus came up immediately from the water; and behold, the heavens were opened to Him, and He saw the Spirit of God descending like a dove and alighting upon Him."[306] The Holy Spirit's descent upon Him in the Jordan River was a descent upon the Faithful, because of His bearing mankind's body. When the Theanthropos, as Man, was washed in the Jordan, it was mankind who was washed in Him and by Him. And when He received the Spirit, it was mankind who by Him were made recipients of the Spirit.[307]

Sealing is done today in the Ecclesia during the Mystery of Chrismation. Holy Myrrh is made up of forty fragrant essences, which symbolize the manifold gifts of the Holy Spirit, which the Believer receives after Baptism. The Presbyter then anoints all of the parts of the Believer's body saying, "The seal of the gift of the Holy Spirit. Amen." This consecrated Myrrh is the confirmation and scal that he who was baptized has received the gifts and charismata of the Holy Spirit.[308]

---

[304] *The Orthodox New Testament*, 2 vol., 2nd ed., Buena Vista, Holy Apostles Convent, 2000, II, 77.

[305] John Chrysostom Homily 4, P.G. 60:33, cited in *Testament*, II, 77.

[306] *Matthew* 3:16

[307] Athanasios the Great, *Four Discourses Against the Arians*, Discourse I, Ch. XII, 47: cited in *Testament*, I, 80.

[308] Frangopoulos, 210.

It is asserted that the Holy Spirit is the author of prophecy. Since He is, then all prophecy must be correct. The success rate of a prophet must be 100% since prophecy comes from the Truth. As Scripture asserts the Faithful are prophets, "For the testimony of Jesus is the spirit of prophecy."[309] Having been given the gifts of the Holy Spirit, the Faithful testify of the words and deeds of the Theanthropos and receiving from that same Holy Spirit the revelation of future events, communicate them to the Faithful and the Ecclesia. In other words, the Spirit of the testimony of Christ is also the Spirit of prophecy, which is, having the same dignity and the same purpose.[310]

Some theologians place a great deal of emphasis on Scripture and how the Holy Spirit is understood as the author, and how He communicates throughout Scripture. There are certain conclusions that require further investigation since interpretation cannot be done in isolation of the Ecclesia. The role of the Ecclesia is confirmed in Scripture: "knowing this first, that no prophecy of Scripture is of any private interpretation."[311] The Holy Spirit manifests Himself outside of the Ecclesia as an outside manifestation. Within the Ecclesia, the Holy Spirit indwells every ethical person.

Theologians, who are proponents of dispensations, suggest that the Holy Spirit functions in a unique way in contemporary time. They assert that this is a time of: intercalation; new purpose; witnessing; non-National entities; evil; gentile; and cosmological. This is based upon a non-scientific supposition.

Since the Holy Spirit is one Hypostasis of the Tri-Hypostatical Divinity it is impossible to have a time of intercalation, since He is omniscient. There can be no new purpose, since He is omnipresent. Witnessing is based upon a supposition that people must do what the

---

[309] *Revelation* 19:10
[310] Averky, 190
[311] 2 *Peter* 1:20

Holy Spirit does. The aspect of Nationhood was previously discussed in Ecclesiology and Eschatology, and the reality of Israel being a Nation Who has a relationship with the Tri-Hypostatical Divinity. The presence of evil is known throughout time but is restricted when a person is obedient to the Ecclesia, Who is guided by the Holy Spirit. There is no gentile today, since the Ecclesia is available to all to accept or reject whether individual or country. The Holy Spirit exercises dominion over the cosmos through the Ecclesia. A more appropriate assertion of contemporary times is theological research under the auspices of the Holy Spirit.

Based upon the source document of 2 *Thessalonians* 2:6-7, some theologians consider the Holy Spirit to be the One who restrains evil in the cosmos. There is no research cited to explain this position. There is much proof to refute this in Eschatological research. One may inquire, what is that which withholds? Some say the Grace of the Holy Spirit, but others that of Roman rule, to which scientific proof agrees. Why? Because if Paul had meant to say the Holy Spirit, he would not have spoken obscurely, but plainly, that even now the Grace of the Holy Spirit, that is the gifts of grace, withhold Him. If he were about to come when the Gifts of Grace cease, he ought now to have come, for they have long ceased. He said this of the Roman rule that is speaking covertly and darkly, not wishing to bring upon him superfluous enmities and senseless dangers. Only there is the one who restrains now, until he comes to be taken out of the midst; that is, whenever the Empire is taken out of the way, then he shall come. For as long as there is fear of the Empire, no one will willingly exult himself. But when that is dissolved, he will attack the anarchy, and endeavour to seize upon the sovereignty both of mankind and the Tri-Hypostatical Divinity.[312]

One of the reasons the Holy Spirit is not possible in the theory of

---

[312] Commentary made by John Chrysostom, Hom. 4, P.G. 62:529, cited in *Testament*, II, 343.

restraining is His acknowledged role of convicting the unregenerate. There is a supposition that during the reign of the Antichrist, the Jewish people will recognize that Jesus of Nazareth is their Messiah. However, how can this possibly happen if the Holy Spirit is not present? To what kind of organism can the Jews become associated with if the Ecclesia is not present upon the Earth? The answer is that the Holy Spirit does convict all to the reality that Jesus of Nazareth is the Theanthropos, whether the person is a Jew or a citizen of any other nationality.

Let us see what research is available to explain the function of the Holy Spirit in relation to those who participate in the Ecclesia. It is abundantly clear that the Ecclesia is a key as we assess the data.

The nous, which has rebelled against the Tri-Hypostatical Divinity, becomes either bestial or unethical and after having rebelled against the laws of nature, lusts after what belong to others. Through the Mystery of Baptism, man's nous is illuminated, freed from slavery to sin, and is united with the Tri-Hypostatical Divinity as a rite of birth. This is why Baptism is called illumination.[313]

Many theologians acknowledge an aspect of the impartation of life for mankind through the Holy Spirit. These are: an understanding of the Tri-Hypostatical Divinity; communication with the Tri-Hypostatical Divinity, commonly referred to as prayer; an understanding of Scripture; recognition of the Ecclesia and; a yearning to share with others. Research recognizes these. So the nous needs therapy, a therapy, which the Fathers of the Ecclesia call quickening, and purifying of the nous. So, purification of the nous and heart is essential. Praxis is purification, and theoria is illumination of the nous and communion with the Tri-Hypostatical Divinity. In any case praxis precedes theoria.[314] Theoria is

---

[313] Hierotheos, *Psychotherapy*, 37, where Gregory Palamas is cited as one authority.
[314] Ibid, 39-40.

the nous' vision; it is to be amazed and to understand all that has been and is to be.[315]

The acquisition of the Holy Spirit is clearly delineated in *The Acquisition of the Holy Spirit in Ancient Russia*.[316]

In every Divine Service (e.g., the Divine Liturgy) the entire Ecclesia is invisibly present, as the true one flock, offering common and unanimous prayers and thanksgiving through the Theanthropos to the Tri-Hypostatical Divinity. This is not a psychological or subjective connection with the past, but the ontological unity of life. In the Ecclesia time ceases, since there is no death, and the interruption of earthly life suspends the living relationship of the generation. The Ecclesia is always contemporary.[317]

Many theologians discuss the induction into the "Family and Household of the Tri-Hypostatical Divinity". This description usually indicates a spiritual conceptualization, rather than the reality of the Ecclesia. There are no proofs presented for any position other than the Ecclesia.

Regeneration relates to the Ecclesia through the position of inheritance of a Son's portion. We read confirmation. Basil, called the Great, asked the Tri-Hypostatical Divinity to enlighten his understanding, so that he might celebrate the offering of the un-bloody sacrifice of the Theanthropos with his own words, and that the Grace of the Holy Spirit might be sent down upon him for this task. When Basil, as the Episcopate had performed this, Ebbulus and the clergy of higher rank (i.e., Presbyters and those of the diaconate) beheld a celestial light illuminating the Sanctuary as well as Basil. In addition certain radiant men clad in white garments (i.e., Ethereal Beings) surrounded

---

[315] Isaac the Syrian cited in Ibid, 40.
[316] I.M. Kontzevitch, *The Acquisition of the Holy Spirit in Ancient Russia*, Platina, St. Herman of Alaska Brotherhood, 1988.
[317] Popovich, 85.

Basil. This is confirmation that the Tri-Hypostatical Divinity blesses the Divine Liturgy According to Saint Basil the Great.[318]

As discussed in Eschatology, we see research presented relating to eternal glory that commences at the coming of the Ecclesia into time.

Faith is the basis of understanding Regeneration. Now in order to be cured it is essential to understand that one is truly ill. When a sick person is unaware of his illness, he cannot turn to a doctor for healing. Self-knowledge is one of the first steps to a cure. The sense of being ill is not enough in itself, however. In any case a therapist is required as well. This therapist is usually one in Holy Orders known as a spiritual father. He who has first been cured of his own ailments or at least is struggling to be cured, and then he can also cure his spiritual children. It is imperative that the spiritual father must be a theologian, and vice versa.[319]

As a result of Regeneration, mankind is eligible to receive the indwelling of the Holy Spirit. This is confirmed in numerous Scripture. This occurs, as discussed above, at the Mystery of Chrismation.

This is a reasonable position, since there is a tremendous amount of proof available through research. Let us consider the Lives of the Saints. We are in the Heavenly Realm, for the Earth becomes the Heavenly Realm through the Saints of the Tri-Hypostatical Divinity. We are among the Ethereal Beings, while still in the flesh, among the Faithful in the Ecclesiastical Community. Whoever they are, the Theanthropos is completely in them, and among them; and there is the whole Eternal Divine Truth, and the whole Eternal Divine Righteousness, and the whole Eternal Divine Love, and the whole Eternal Divine Life.[320]

This is what the Saints see when they behold the Holy Spirit:

---

[318] *The Lives of the Three Great Hierarchs*, 24-25
[319] Hierotheos, *Psychotherapy*, 44
[320] Popovich, 42-43

There are many theologians who accept the relation of the sealing to a type of mystical experience that has no observable elements. This is based upon biblical theology, without utilizing scientific methodologies of research.

Among some theologians there are varied interpretations with reference to "the Baptism of the Holy Spirit." There are some theologians who feel that this is water baptism and argue what the proper mode is. This is interesting, but they fail to provide appropriate data. Other theologians feel that this is related to a concept called sanctification, which comes after regeneration. Again, there is no research to prove their positions.

Both theological positions prove totally inadequate when ascertaining proofs utilizing scientific data. Data is provided in the book *Orthodoxy and the Religion of the Future*. Some conclusions are below.

Those who bring theological ideas to the experience make the assumption that the "Baptism in the Holy Spirit" must be a Christian experience. The very possibility of an experience of a "Pentecost without Christ" means that the experience in itself is not Christian at all. Christians, often sincere and well-meaning, are reading into the experience a Christian content which in itself it does not have.[321]

The life of self-centredness and self-satisfaction lived by most of today's Christians is so all-pervading that it effectively seals them off from any understanding at all of spiritual life; when such people do undertake any type of spiritual life, it is only as another form of self-satisfaction. This can be seen quite clearly in the totally false religious ideal both of the Charismatic Movement and the various forms of Christian meditation: all of them promise, and give very quickly, an experience of contentment and peace.[322]

In the Western European society, to be sure, the Grace of the Tri-Hypostatical Divinity was lost many centuries ago. The followers of the Popes of Rome and the Reformation today have not tasted of the Grace of the Tri-Hypostatical Divinity, and so it is not surprising that they should be unable to discern its demonic counterfeit.[323]

Some theologians speak about the believer's responsibilities, which are described as: motivation, obligation, and dependency. This is proposed in light of *The Orthodox Study Bible*, as asserted in the reality of spiritual transformation. There is much discussion about the terms of reference. The latter is the weakness of biblical theology. There is an obvious aspect of responsibility of a Believer, who receives Regeneration, predominantly to participate in the Ecclesia.

The Holy Spirit provides power to overcome evil, as some theologians assert. They divide evil into three categories: the world, the flesh, and the devil. Research indicates that only Satan is the source of evil. Research indicates that Satan has an independent personality, but in the long run loses since there is no power. Even when he causes

---

[321] Seraphim Rose, *Orthodoxy and the Religion of the Future*, Platina, Saint Herman of Alaska Brotherhood, 1990, 207.

[322] Ibid, 223

[323] Ibid, 225

some terrible thing, such as the Russian Revolution, out of it come the New Martyrs, a tremendous inspiration for mankind.[324]

The Holy Spirit allows mankind to be beneficial. Research indicates that in the Ecclesia and the disciples know action is chiefly purification of the heart, and theoria is noetic prayer and the vision of the uncreated Light, the theosis of mankind. Action needs to be learned and theoria put into practice.[325]

Research relating to the nous states, when it enters the condition contrary to nature, it forgets the justice that comes from the Tri-Hypostatical Divinity and fights with mankind, believing that they are unjustly treated. When the nous is raised to the state above nature, it finds the fruits of the Holy Spirit.[326] The fruit of the Spirit is love, joy, peace, longsuffering, kindness, goodness, faithfulness, gentleness, self-control.[327]

It is generally acknowledged that The Holy Spirit grants gifts to mankind. This is most pronounced in the services of the Ecclesia. The most pertinent is in the area of praise, thanksgiving, teaching, and leading. This is observable in the numerous Lives of the Saints.

With reference to the Life of Faith and the Intercession of the Spirit, the Life of St. John of San Francisco is most pertinent. Among the books on his Life, *Blessed John the Wonderworker*[328] is one of the best. St. John's incorrupt relics lie in a glass casket for all to observe in the Cathedral of All Sorrows in San Francisco. The author confirms this through personal observation, and challenges any who are sceptical to go and see for themselves.

Some theologians point to Scripture that cites, "do not grieve the

---

[324] Rose, *Genesis*, 490
[325] Hierotheos, *Mind*, 155
[326] Hierotheos, *Psychotherapy*, 127
[327] Galatians 5:22, 23
[328] Seraphim Rose and Herman, *Blessed John*.

Holy Spirit of God,"[329] and "do not quench the Spirit."[330] It is not possible to prove negative suppositions utilizing scientific methodologies. Research does indicate the positive attitudes toward these Scriptural passages. Theosis is the answer to the positive proof required. Theosis, which is the goal of the ethical life, is a manifestation of the Tri-Hypostatical Divinity to the pure heart of mankind. This vision of the uncreated Light is what creates spiritual delight in mankind's nous.[331]

Some theologians often describe this venture as a "Walk in the Spirit". Research indicates how this venture commences. Illumination, that is the Mystery of Baptism, is the radiance of souls, the change of life, intercession to the Tri-Hypostatical Divinity that He may grant each Believer a good conscience; illumination is an aid to our spiritual weakness; illumination is a shaking off of our carnal mind; it is the following of the Spirit, Communion with the Theanthropos as Logos, the correction of mankind, the destruction of sin, the participation in light, the abrogation of darkness. Illumination is the vehicle, which transports us to the Tri-Hypostatical Divinity, a co-journeying to the Theanthropos, a foundation of faith, and a key to the Heavenly Realm.[332]

Much of the role of the Holy Spirit has relationship to His role in the Creation. Research indicates the Holy Spirit fittingly moves over the Earth, destined to bear fruit, because by the aid of the Spirit it held the seeds of new birth which were to germinate according to the words of the Prophet, "You send forth Your Spirit, they are created; And You renew the face of the earth."[333] [334]

---

[329] Ephesians 4:30
[330] 1 Thessalonians 5:19
[331] Hierotheos, *Psychotherapy*, 353
[332] Gregory the Theologian cited by Frangopoulos, 209
[333] Psalm 104:30
[334] Ambrose of Milan cited by Rose, *Genesis*, 109

We see research utilizing scientific methodologies to confirm the Holy Spirit and His role. Discipleship comes through the Holy Spirit.

The Truth can be understood when one comes to realize that the Truth is one Hypostasis of the Tri-Hypostatical Divinity. The Holy Spirit provides the power to understand the Truth. Without this power it is impossible to become a disciple among the Theanthropic Saints.

Eschatology

Theologians should see eschatology as one of the most relevant areas of research, since it is essential to be knowledgeable of the results for everyone and everything.

Many theologians only study Eschatology with reference to Scripture alone. Depending upon the faith group, the theologians make their conclusions without reference to individuals. This is referred to as Cosmic Eschatology.

The Cosmic Eschatological research has been clearly defined by J. Warner Wallace utilizing forensic science.[335] He proves that Jesus of Nazareth is God Incarnate.

Creation reaches her normal state upon her culmination since Grace is implied in the Theanthropos' Act of Creation. Deification is the final result of Creation.[336]

We are evaluating within the context of individual eschatological research since this can be studied thoroughly, due to people dying on a daily basis.

---

[335] J. Warner Wallace, *Person of Interest*, Grand Rapids, Zondervan Reflective, 2021.
[336] Lossky, 101

The views of scientific theological positions can be evaluated based upon Individual Eschatology.

There are two principal Christian Cosmic Eschatological positions based primarily upon the *Apocalypse*[337] found in *The Orthodox Study Bible*. These two are generally referred to as: Historicist and Futurist positions.

The most extensive research of the Book of Revelation could be found in Volume 1 of the Theanthropic Ethical category book entitled, **POWER Living** *Through Revelation*.[338] This is being updated as *Revelation: The Definitive position*, which will be published soon.

The only Cosmic Eschatological position that has any relationship to Individual Eschatology, and scientific data is the definitive position.

It is appropriate to evaluate the Historicist and Futurist positions before evaluating the Definitive position. The Historicist and Futurist positions are based upon the concept of numerous dispensations.

The concept of dispensations asserts that specific eras involve different methodologies for the Tri-Hypostatical Divinity to deal with mankind. A basic supposition is that Israel has a special relationship to the extent that the Tri-Hypostatical Divinity owes something to Israel as a nation.

The Historicist position is based upon the supposition that the Pope of Rome or the papacy is the Antichrist, as described in the *Apocalypse*. This is the basis of the Reformation movement in the Middle Ages.

The Futurist position contends that there is a future Antichrist. This is also based upon the *Apocalypse*. The difference between the Futurist and Definitive positions is the theory of chiliasm. The Futurist position asserts that chiliasm is a viable theory. This is based upon the fact that chiliasm was acknowledged by many theologians up to the third

---

[337] This is referred to as *Revelation* in other areas of this book.
[338] This is my book that describes the Book of Revelation from a scientific perspective.

century. There were even a few theologians who supported the theory of chiliasm into the fourth century.[339]

Chiliasm is based primarily upon *Apocalypse* 20:1-6. Chiliasm is similar to the theory of an "Age of Aquarius" in many apocalyptic theories of various faith groups. Chiliasm differs only to the extent that there is a literal millennium of time. Some faith groups utilise the term Millennium, but do not subscribe to the idea of a literal time frame.

The theory of Chiliasm is a literal and physical 1,000 year reign of Jesus, who as King of Israel reinstates the Mosaic Law.[340]

Chiliasm is considered important to those who hold the Futurist position who subscribe to Israel as a special kingdom utilising the dispensational theory.

The concept goes as follows. The Theanthropos failed to provide a Messianic Kingdom on His first Advent. The result is that He must return and provide the appropriate kingdom for Israel.

The Definitive position is based upon scientific methodologies. The first evaluation is to ascertain who the recipients were of *the Apocalypse*. It is clear that the recipients are the seven Episcopates of the Ecclesia. The next evaluation is to ascertain if the message has been continuously understood by the Ecclesia. Data indicates that there is an unbroken understanding from the Ecclesia, since She is an Eternal Organism. In addition, this refutes the reality of Pentecost, which is celebrated every year throughout the Ecclesia. This occurs 50 days after Pascha, the formula for which is decreed by Jesus the Theanthropos and confirmed through the Holy Fire.[341] [342]

As in all scientific disciplines a theory must be proven. The

---

[339] Chafer, IV, 270-7

[340] Keen, 243. Refer to 243-245 for the reasons why the theory of Chiliasm is rejected.

[341] The Holy Fire in Scripture, History, and Science" Presented by David DiPuccio, Ph.D. https://www.youtube.com/watch?v=dhOsZXtKK3w&t=40s

[342] Keen, *Applied Business Ethics, Volume 1: **POWER Living** Through the Truth*. Bloomington, iUniverse, 2012, 257-258

theory of chiliasm was a working hypothesis. The Ecclesia rejects this theory in 381 at the Second Ecumenical Council. She clarifies the correct understanding at the same time, since this is confirmed by the introduction into the Symbol of Faith of the words "whose Kingdom shall have no end."[343] [344]

The *Apocalypse* is highly controversial as to the appropriate interpretation. The *Apocalypse* is confusing to those who do not recognize the Ecclesia. The author of the *Apocalypse* is the only Head of the Ecclesia; the Theanthropos Who sends this text to the Ecclesia. This is one of the few *Books* of *The Orthodox Study Bible* that contains a promise to understand the text. This is a basic *Book* in the Ecclesia. Anyone who checks out *Apocalypse* 1:3 can see the reality of understanding this Message from the Theanthropos to His Ecclesia.[345]

Perhaps part of the problem is that the *Apocalypse* confirms the relationships contained in the Ecclesia. If one attempts to understand the *Apocalypse* without this conceptualization of the physical presence of the Ecclesia, then it becomes incredibly difficult.

Few theologians, who have problems understanding the *Apocalypse*, have bothered to seek out the Ecclesiastical Communities who are the recipients of this document. Some of the Ecclesiastical Communities exist to this day.[346] This is due to Conciliar nature of the Ecclesia. Every decision in Councils is ratified by all of the Ecclesiastical Communities throughout the world.

With reference to the *Apocalypse* the Definitive position is the understanding of the Ecclesia, be it the seven recipients or the Ecumenical Ecclesia. A complete understanding can be found in *The*

---

[343] +Jonah, 61.

[344] Averky, 201

[345] For a thorough review check Averky, 44

[346] Averky,.58

Apocalypse in the Teachings of Ancient Christianity,[347]or **POWER Living Through Revelation**.[348] Watch for the upcoming book, *Revelation: the Definitive position* for further research.

Individual Eschatology can be evaluated, since people die every day. There are numerous accounts of "after death experiences" that assist theologians in evaluating the data.

Mankind is a psychosomatic being, which means that neither the nous nor the body constitutes the whole of a person. So, at the moment when the nous is separated from the body by death, mystifying things take place. The nous was not living before the creation of the body; therefore, it does not want to live without it. The nous' departure from the body is by force, and this is the mystery of death.[349]

Many of the sources within the realm of Individual Eschatology come from centuries of research. One of the oldest, most comprehensive is a Buddhist text entitled, *The Tibetan Book of the Dead*.[350] This is an eighth century text, originally entitled, *Liberation by Hearing on the After-Death Plane*. In addition, there is the ancient Egyptian text entitled, *The Book of the Dead*.[351] These are similar in their content.

There are many theories relating to Eschatology. Some theologians make the supposition that mankind may go into non-existence, while others that the union of the nous and bodies is broken definitely, and does not speak of the resurrection of bodies and the reuniting of the nous and body. Other theologians ascribe to the nous union with other bodies, since, as the supposition goes, the nous are also linked with other incarnations, in accordance with the theory of metensarcosis of the soul or metempsychosis of the body. Others regard the next life

---

[347] Averky
[348] Keen
[349] Hierotheos, *Life*,52
[350] W.Y. Evans-Wentz (ed.) *The Book of the Dead*, Oxford University Press, 1960.
[351] E.A. Wallis Budge (tr.), Bell Publishing Co., N.Y., 1960, cited Rose, *Soul*, 91,

as similar to the present one, since they theorize; those equal to the Ethereal Beings have food suitable for a perishable life. Chiliasts belong to the latter category.[352]

Research indicates that there is much relevance to *The Tibetan Book of the Dead*. Dr. C.G. Jung, in his Psychological Commentary on the book, finds these visions very similar to descriptions of the after-death world in the spiritualistic literature of the modern West – both give one a sickening impression of the utter inanity and banality of the communications from the spirit world.[353]

In two respects there are striking similarities between the *Tibetan Book of the Dead* and today's experiences, and this account, for the interest of Dr. Moody and other researchers in this book. First, the out-of-body experience describes in the first moments of death is essentially the same as that described in today's experiences, as well as in data, that is the nous of the deceased appears as a shining illusory body, which is visible to other beings of like nature but not men in the flesh. At first the person does not know whether they are alive or dead; they see people around the body, hear the wailing of mourners, and have all sense faculties; they have unimpeded motion and proceed through solid objects.[354] Second, there is a primary clear light seen at the moment of death,[355] which today's researchers identify with the being of light described by many people today.[356]

Research indicates that different people, depending upon their expectations, understand this being of light as diverse personages. For example, many dying Hindus see the gods of their Hindu Pantheon,

---

[352] Hierotheos, *Life*, 82
[353] Rose, *Soul*, 99
[354] Ibid, 98-100, 156-160
[355] Ibid, 89
[356] Ibid, 99

such as Krishna, Shiva, Kali, etc., rather than those close relatives and friends commonly reported in America.[357]

This being of light can be understood, when we consider the conclusions made by research. Since the nous is noetic, yet not spiritual as is the Tri-Hypostatical Divinity, therefore is created and ethereal. Just as Ethereal Beings, although they are ministering spirits, are called ethereal beings, so also mankind's nous is ethereal. In this sense research indicates that after the nous leaves the body the Ethereal Beings or demonic Ethereal Beings receive them.[358] Whether an individual's nous is received by good or evil Ethereal Beings is based upon the lifestyle of the individual.

The death of non-Believers in the Ecclesia has been recorded. The death of Joseph Stalin, a contemporary apostate, atheist, cold-blooded criminal and merciless persecutor of the Ecclesia is highly characteristic. His daughter, Svetlana, in her memoirs, describes the agony and the terror of the last moments: She writes:

"'My father died a difficult and terrible death. It was the first and so far the only time I have seen somebody die. God grants an easy death only to the just.

'The hemorraging had gradually spread to the rest of his brain. Since his heart was healthy and strong, it affected the breathing centers bit by bit and caused suffocation. His breathing became shorter and shorter. For the last twelve hours the lack of oxygen was acute. His face altered and became dark. His lips turned black and the features grew unrecognizable. The last hours were nothing but a slow strangulation. The death agony was horrible. He literally choked to death as we watched. At what seemed like the very last moment he suddenly opened his eyes and cast a glance over everyone in the room. It was a terrible glance,

---

[357] Ibid, 26
[358] Hierotheos, *Life*, 81

insane or perhaps angry and full of the fear of death and the unfamiliar faces of the doctors bent over him. The glance swept over everyone in a second. Then something incomprehensible and awesome happened that to this day I can't forget and don't understand. He suddenly lifted his left hand as though he were pointing to something above and bringing down a curse on us all. The gesture was incomprehensible and full of menace, and no one could say to whom or at what it might be directed. The next moment, after a final effort, the spirit wretched itself free of the flesh."[359]

How different is the death of one who is a Member of the Ecclesia. The death of Sava the first Archbishop of Serbia is recounted below.

"Thereafter, Sava took Holy Communion and then still continued to pray, in a whispering voice, for many persons and nations by name, and for those he had known in the past, and for those unknown to him in the future.

"Then at dawn of the following day, January 14, 1235, the watching disciples heard a mysterious voice say:

"'Rejoice, my servant, lover of truth!' And a little later again:

"'Come, my good and faithful servant, receive the rewards which I have promised to all who love me.'

"At that moment, Sava smiled with joy, and gave up his holy soul to God. The disciples quickly put a burning candle at his head according to an ancient custom, and crossed his hands over his breast. Such was the separation from the body of a soul destined for immortal life and glory."[360]

There is numerous data confirming the reality of "tollhouses" substantiated by research. The research relating to the twenty torments

---

[359] Svetlana Alleluyeva, *Twenty Letters to a Friend*. New York, McMillan, Harper & Row, Publishers, 1967, 10, cited by Vassiliadis,333-334.
[360] Velimirovich, *Life*, 147-148.

(i.e., tollhouses) can be found in *Eternal Mysteries Beyond the Grave*,[361] Chapter 14.

All demonic Ethereal Beings act with malice against mankind, since they would like to dominate everyone and have them in their power forever. It is impossible for these demonic Ethereal Beings to have authority over the righteous.[362]

The Heavenly Realm becomes the natural habitation for mankind as long as he/she is righteous, just as Paradise is mankind's natural habitation. Mankind exists in an unnatural habitation today.

Satan and his demonic Ethereal Beings have caused the removal of mankind from Paradise and now desire to remove mankind from the Heavenly Realm.

What is the Heavenly Realm like? It is very clear from research that fire has relevance.

Fire has two powers, caustic and illuminating energies, and consequently burns and sheds light. Those worthy of the fire will feel its caustic quality and those worthy of this type of lighting will feel the illuminating property of the fire.

The fire of Hell will be dark, it will be deprived of the illuminating quality, while the light of the righteous will be caustic, without the burning quality, and this will be the result of a different energy of the Tri-Hypostatical Divinity. Nevertheless, this suggests that according to his condition a person may receive the uncreated energy of the Tri-Hypostatical Divinity.[363]

Does the Ecclesia hold any hope for all mankind?

As we have seen in Soteriology the Heavenly Realm may be

---

[361] Panteleimon, *Eternal_Mysteries Beyond the Grave*, Jordanville, Holy Trinity Monastery, 1996.
[362] Hierotheos, *Life*, 64
[363] Basil the Great cited by Hierotheos, *Life*, 257

experienced now. This means that the Ecclesia, as an Eternal Organism, has the answer.

The Ecclesia has special Memorials for the repose of Her faithful members. She prays for the Faithful on the third, ninth, and fortieth day after death. The third day the Ecclesia remembers the Resurrection on the third day of the Theanthropos, so She prays to Him to resurrect the reposed to the future life of blessedness. The ninth day the Ecclesia remembers the Ethereal Beings, who are distinguished by their nine orders, so She prays to the Theanthropos for the reposed to be reckoned among the choir pleasing to the Tri-Hypostatical Divinity. The fortieth day the Ecclesia remembers the Theanthropos' Ascension into the Heavenly Realm, so She prays to the Theanthropos that the reposed may be lifted up into the Heavenly Realm.

Due to the love and faith of the relatives, often the remembrance of the reposed is celebrated on every one of the forty days with the serving of the Divine Liturgy and a Memorial Service.

On the anniversary of the repose of the deceased, close relatives and faithful friends pray for the reposed as an expression of their faith that the day of a human death is not the day of annihilation, but a new rebirth to eternal life. It is the day of the passing of the immortal human soul into different conditions of life, where there is no place for earthly pains, grief, and woes.

Memorial Services are short services, which consist of prayers for the forgiveness of sins and the repose of the deceased in the Heavenly Realm. During the serving of the Memorial Service, relatives and friends of the deceased stand with their lit candles which are symbolic of the future, radiant life. Towards the end of the Memorial Service, during the reading of the Lord's Prayer, these candles are extinguished as a sign that our lives, like burning candles, must expire, more often than not without burning through to the expected end.[364]

For the unbelievers, there is little hope. Only private prayers can be said. An example of this type of prayer is: "Have mercy, O Lord, if it be possible, on the soul of Thy slave (name) who has departed into eternal life in separation from Thy Holy Orthodox Church! Unsearchable are Thy decrees. Do not account this my prayer as a sin, but may Thy holy will be done!"[365]

Research indicates the close relationship between Ecclesiology and Eschatology.

New Data:

The Truth understands the eschatological repercussions of failure to maintain ethical standards.

Metropolitan Hilarion presents in his book, *Christ the Conqueror of Death* [366] presents the scientifically verifiable facts of Christ's descent into Hades. There is very comprehensive data supplied from 234 sources.

His Eminence Metropolitan Joseph offers the Endorsement of *The Departure of the Soul According to the Teaching of the Orthodox Church* [367] regarding the reality of Toll Houses when people die, which falls into the scientific study of Eschatology. This book is endorsed by numerous Hierarches throughout the world. Within the 8 chapters consisting of numerous confirmable facts from various studies. There are 989 pages not including Appendices! There are also numerous Academic Endorsements.

---

[364] Slobodskoy, 594

[365] Rose, *Soul*, 225

[366] Metropolitan Hilarion,. *Christ the Conqueror of Death*. Crestwood, St. Vladimir's Seminary Press, 2009.

[367] +Joseph, Metropolitan, *The Departure of the Soul According to the Teaching of the Orthodox Church*. Florence, St. Anthony's Greek Orthodox Monastery, 2017.

Conclusion

The supposition for theology – that there is a god or gods – is proven. Theology is a scientific discipline.

The basic proofs are given in Chapter 1. These are irrefutable.

There is overwhelming proof that the supposition is true due to the availability of numerous basic extrapolated data. This is scientifically verifiable data that is resultant only through the reality that theology is a scientific discipline.

This research was presented as a doctoral thesis entitled *Theology As A Scientific Discipline.* The Examining Committee consisted of Dr. Steven A. Shuemake as Chairman and Dr. Carl W. Warden as Dean for Bethany Divinity College and Seminary. The Examining Committee examined the thesis for my Doctor of Theological Studies and found it to be acceptable. Dr. Edison E. Wiltshire, Director of Canadian Affairs for Bethany Divinity College and Seminary chaired the dissertation.

I published my doctoral thesis 2010 with iUniverse. To my knowledge nobody in the world could refute the fact that theology **is** a Scientific Discipline. More research over the years has confirmed this reality. In addition, the Russian Federation has mandated that tertiary level educational facilities include theology as a science course.

Date of Pascha

One of the greatest areas of research is the determination of the date of Pascha. This is confirmed by the Mother Ecclesiastical Community of Jerusalem through the Miraculous Occurrence of the Holy Fire. The reception of the Holy Light comes only to the correct Episcopate of the Mother Ecclesiastical Community.

The date of Pascha is determined by a formula, so it is easy to determine the correct day. Despite this recurring annual Miraculous Occurrence, people refuse to accept this reality.

Why is it so relevant to know this date?

Anyone can go to Jerusalem on the specific date and receive the Holy Fire within the precincts of the Temple of the Resurrection of Christ. This is truly an opportunity to experience a Miraculous Occurrence. This is easily verifiable by attending and observing. Many people have photographed and videotaped the Holy Light.

Scientific Criteria

Scientific criteria have been maintained throughout. Proofs have been supplied for the basic supposition of: there is a god or gods. In order to refute this supposition scientifically, then one must provide another supposition.

The extrapolated data have provided additional proofs for the supposition. These proofs should be assessed utilizing objective criteria. This is the true methodology of scientific research.

Consequently, the Theanthropic Ethical category is based upon the scientific discipline of Theology. This is extremely relevant, yet this is only the starting point.

Remember, this entire book is just about the supposition. There is far more to come.

Already the Theanthropic Nation of Russia has endorsed the reality that theology is a scientific discipline for all tertiary level educational facilities! Theologians throughout the world teach theology utilizing scientific research. Recognition is the next stage for all tertiary level institutions at the very least.

The Rudder

The Rudder is one of the greatest ways to implement governance. When I first heard of the huge book it was endorsed by our Chief Hierarch, +David, Bishop of Altoona. He encouraged all under Holy Orders to read *The Rudder*.

I have read it so many times I have lost track of how many times. I have it thoroughly about 6 times with footnotes, etc. It was a daunting task since some of the references were about 3 or 4 pages later. I really never realised the significance of the rudder on a ship.

My first experience was when I was going a short trip across to Centre Island from the Toronto docks on a ferry. The captain of the ferry was taking a break, so I asked him how important a rudder was on the ferry. He told me, "If we didn't have a rudder, we would miss Centre Island!" This was amazing to me because one could see the dock on the island. He said, "There is a strong current so we would miss it."

A few years later I purchased a DVD of the movie, "Sink the Bismarck" and I realized that one biplane in Royal Air Force (RAF) stopped the Bismarck by sending a torpedo that smashed the rudder. Wow!

I realize now that *The Rudder* is an exceptional book of the Canons of the Ecclesia. There is the benefit of flexibility which allows all of Christ's disciples to persevere in the Truth according to their particular circumstances.

Bibliography

The Holy Bible. London, Her Majesty's Printer, 1611.

Ethiopian Bible in English Complete, Blue Nile Spiritual Texts, 2024

The Orthodox Study Bible. Nashville, Thomas Nelson, 2008

The Orthodox New Testament. 2 vol., 2nd ed. Buena Vista, Holy Apostles Convent, 2000.

The Life of the Virgin Mary, the Theotokos. Buena Vista, Holy Apostles Convent, 1989.

The Lives of the Three Great Hierarchs: Basil the Great, Gregory the Theologian, and John Chrysostom. Buena Vista, Dormition Skete, 1985.

The Lives of the Monastery Builders of the Holy Mountain Athos. Buena Vista, Holy Apostles Convent, 1992.

Aleksiev, Archimandrite Seraphim. *The Forgotten Medicine*. Wildwood, St. Xenia Skete, 1994.

Alfeyen, Metropolitan Hilarion. *Christ the Conqueror of Death*. Crestwood, St. Vladimir's Seminary Press, 2009.

Augustine, St., Bishop of Hippo. *Confessions*. London, The Folio Society, 1993.

Averky, Archbishop, of Jordanville. *The Apocalypse of St. John: An Orthodox Commentary*. Platina., St. Herman of Alaska Brotherhood, 1985.

Bakogiannis, Archimandrite Vasilios. *After Death*. Katerini, Tertios Publications, 1995.

Basil, St., the Great. *On The Holy Spirit*. Crestwood, St. Vladimir's Seminary Press, 1980.

Cabasilas, Nicholas. *A Commentary on the Divine Liturgy*. London, S.P.C.K., 1983.

Cabasilas, Nicholas. *The Life in Christ*. Crestwood, St. Vladimir's Seminary Press, 1974.

Cavarnos, Constantine and Zeldin, Mary-Barbara. *St. Seraphim of Sarov*. Belmont, Institute for Byzantine and Modern Greek Studies, 1980

Chafer, Lewis Sperry. *Systematic Theology*, 8 Vol. Grand Rapids, Kregel Publications, 1976.

Doder, Protopresbyter-Stavrophor Mihajlo. *Vespers For The Sunday of Orthodoxy*. Mississauga, All Serbian Saints Serbian Orthodox Church, 2003.

Enoch. *The Book of Enoch*. Oxford, Clarendon Press, 1912.

Eusebius. *The History of the Church*. Toronto, Penguin Books Canada Ltd., 1989.

Evans=Wentz, W.Y. *The Tibetan Book of the Dead*. Oxford, Oxford University Press, 1960.

Field, Anne. *From Darkness to Light*. Bon Lomond, Conciliar Press, 1997.

Frangopoulos, Athanasios S. *Our Orthodox Christian Faith*, Athens, The Brotherhood of Theologians, 1988.

Geisler, Norman L., ed. *Inerrancy*. Grand Rapids, Zondervan Publishing House, 1980.

Hardy, Edward R., ed. *Christology of the Later Fathers*. Philadelphia, the Westminster Press, 1954.

Hierotheos, Metropolitan of Nafpaktos. *Empirical Dogmatics, Volume 1, According to the Spoken Teaching of Father John Romanides, Dogma-Ethics-Revelation*. Levadia, Birth of the Theotokos Monastery, 2012.

Hierotheos, Metropolitan of Nafpaktos. *Empirical Dogmatics, Volume 2, According to the Spoken Teaching of Father John Romanides, Holy Trinity, Creation, Fall, Incarnation, Church, Life After Death*, 2013.

Hierotheos, Metropolitan of Nafpaktos. *The Illness and Cutr of the Soul in the Orthodox Tradition*. Levadia, Birth of the Theotokos Monastery, 2010.

Hierotheos, Metropolitan of Nafpaktos. *Life After Death*. Levadia, Birth of the Theotokos Monastery, 1996.

Hierotheos, Metropolitan of Nafpaktos. *The Mind of the Orthodox Church*, Levadia, Birth of the Theotokos Monastery, 1998.

Hierotheos, Metropolitan of Nafpaktos. *Orthodox Psychotherapy*. Levadia, Birth of the Theotokos Monastery, 1995.

Hopko, Thomas. *Speaking the Truth in Love*. Crestwood, St. Vladimir's Seminary Press, 2004.

Irenaeus, St. *Proof of the Apostolic Preaching*. New York, Newman Press, 1952.

Jeffreys, Peter. *Saint George's Greek Orthodox Church: An Architectural and Iconographic Guide*. Toronto, University of Toronto Press Inc., 2000.

+Jonah. Archbishop of Washington, Metropolitan of All America and Canada. *The Service Books of the Orthodox Church*. South Canaan, St. Tikhon's Seminary Press, 2010.

+Joseph, Metropolitan. *The Departure of the Soul According to the Teaching of the Orthodox Church*. Florence, St. Anthony's Greek Orthodox Monastery, 2017.

Keen, Dr. Brian. *Applied Business Ethics, Volume 1: **POWER Living** Through the Truth*. Bloomington, iUniverse, 2012.

Keen, Dr. Brian. ***POWER Living** Through Revelation*. Scarborough, The Ethics Institute, 2009.

Keiser, Michael. *Spread the Word*. Chesterton, Conciliar Press, 2011.

Kontzevitch, I.M. *The Acquisition of the Holy Spirit in Ancient Russia*. Platina, St. Herman of Alaska Brotherhood, 1988.

Lossky, Vladimir. *The Mystical Theology of the Eastern Church*. Crestwood, St. Vladimir's Seminary Press, 1957

Mitrofan, Monk Father. *Holy Russia Inside the Soviet Union*. Minneapolis, Light and Life Publishing Co., 1989.

Monk, A. *These Truths We Hold*. South Canaan, St. Tikhon's Seminary Press, 1986.

Nektarios, Bishop of Pentapolis. *Christology*. Roscoe, Saint Nektarios Monastery Publications, 2006.

Nicodemus, Saints, and Agapius. *The Rudder*. West Brookfield, The Orthodox Christian Educational Society, 1983.

Panteleimon, Archimandrite. *Eternal Mysteries Beyond the Grave*. Jordanville, Holy Trinity Monastery, 1996.

Philip, Metropolitan. *Service Book*. Englewood Hills, Antiochian Orthodox Christian Archdiocese of North America, 1984.

Photios of Constantinople. *The Patriarch and the Prince*. Brookline, Holy Cross Orthodox Press, 1982.

Plaut, W. Gunther, ed. *The Torah: A Modern Commentary*. New York, Union of American Hebrew Congregations, 1981.

Pomazansky, Protopresbyter Michael. *Orthodox Dogmatic Theology*, Third Edition. Platina, Saint Herman of Alaska Brotherhood, 2005.

Popovich, Father Justin. *Orthodox Faith and Life in Christ*. Belmont, The Institute for Byzantine and Modern Greek Studies, 1994.

Radovanovic, Marina. *The Noble's Pauper Children*. Baltimore, PublishAmerica, 2005.

Rogich, Daniel. *Serbian Patericon*, 1, Platina, St. Herman of Alaska Brotherhood, 1994/

Rose, Eugene. *Nihilism*. (Second Edition, Third Printing) Platina, St. Herman of Alaska Brotherhood, 2001.

Rose, Fr. Seraphim. *The Soul After Death*, Fourth Edition. Platina, St. Herman of Alaska Brotherhood, 2004.

Rose, Fr. Seraphim and Herman, Abbot. *Blessed John the Wonderworker*. Platina, St. Herman of Alaska Brotherhood, 1987.

Rose, Hieromonk Seraphim. *Genesis, Creation and Early Man*, Platina, St. Herman of Alaska Brotherhood, 2000.

Rose, Hieromonk Seraphim. *Orthodoxy and the Religion of the Future*. Platina, Saint Herman of Alaska Brotherhood, 1990.

Schaeffer, Frank. *Dancing Alone*. Brookline, Holy Cross Orthodox Press, 1994.

Shevkunov, Archimandrite Tikhon. *Everyday Saints and Other Stories*. Dallas, Pokrov Publications, 2012.

Slobodskoy, Archpriest Seraphim. *The Law of God*. Jordanville, Holy Trinity Monastery, 1996.

Sophrony, Archimandrite. *His Life is Mine*. Oxford, A.R. Mowbray & Co. Ltd., 1977.

Sproul, R.C., Gerstner, John, and Lindsley, Arthur. *Classical Apologetics*. Grand Rapids, Zondervan Publishing House, 1984.

Stefanatos, Joanne, D.V.M. *Animals and Man: A State of Blessedness*. Minneapolis, Light and Life Publishing Company, 1992.

Strickland, John. *The Making of Holy Russia*. Jordanville, Holy Trinity Seminary Press, 2013.

Symeon, St., the New Theologian. *The First-Created Man*. Platina, St. Herman of Alaska Brotherhood, 1994.

Symeon, St., the New Theologian. *On The Mystical Life: The Ethical Discourses*, 3 vol., Crestwood, St. Vladimir's Seminary Press, 1995.

Theophylact, Blessed, Archbishop of Ochrid and Bulgaria. *The Explanation of the Holy Gospel According to St. Matthew*. House Springs, Chrysostom Press, 1993.

Vassiliadis, Nikolaos P. *The Mystery of Death*. Athens, The Orthodox Brotherhood of Theologians, 1993.

Velimirovich, Nicholai. *The Life of St. Sava*. Crestwood, Saint Vladimir's Seminary Press, 1989.

Velimirovich, Nikolai, Bishop. *The Faith of Chosen People*. Grayslake, The Free Serbian Orthodox Diocese of America and Canada, 1988.

Wallace, J. Warner. *Cold-Case Christianity*, Updated & Extended Edition, Colorada Springs, David C. Cook, 2023.

Wallace, J. Warner. *Forensic Faith*. Colorada Springs, David C. Cook, 2017

Wallace, J. Warner. *Person of Interest*. Grand Rapids, Zondervan Reflective, 2021.

Wallace, J. Warner. *The Truth in True Crime*. Grand Rapids, Zondervan Reflective, 2024.

Young, Archpriest Alexey. *The Rush to Embrace*. Richfield Springs, Nikodemos Orthodox Publication Society, 1996.

DVDs

Christian Broadcasting Network, The: Made in Israel©2015

Orthodox Spiritualty Series 2005: Hieromonk Ambrose, "Orthodoxy & The Challenge of Our Times" and Mother Theadelphi, "The Scandal of Gender".

Orthodox Spiritualty Series 2007: Hieromonk Damascene, "On Humility" and "The Life and Works of Father Seraphim Rose."

Orthodox Spiritualty Series 2008: Father Daniel Byantoro, "Orthodoxy in the Islamic World."

Orthodox Spiritualty Series 2009: Father Michael Oleksa, "In the Steps of the Saints: Missionaries and Miracle Workers of North America,"

Orthodox Spiritualty Series 2010: Archimandrite Deiniol, "Desert Holiness & Monastic Saints: Orthodox Christianity in Celtic Wales."

Orthodox Spiritualty Series 2011: Fr. Jacob Myers, "The Miracle Working Relics of Christ's Holy Saints."

Orthodox Spiritualty Series 2015: Hieromonk James (Corazza), "A Life of Your Own in Christ: Navigating the Pitfalls of Contemporary Life through the example of the holy life of St John Maximovitch."

Patterns of Evidence: Exodus ©2015

Patterns of Evidence: The Moses Controversy ©2019

Patterns of Evidence: The Israel Dilemma ©2024

Videos

David Rohl "In Search of Eden" https://www.youtube.com/watch?v=xVoggCHlwPw

Erin Go Bragh Pronunciation https://www.youtube.com/watch?v=NoTQuwO3Z0o

Holy Fire, "The: Presented by David DiPuccio, Ph.D. The Holy Fire in Scripture, History, and Science" https://www.youtube.com/watch?v=dhOsZXtKK3w&t=40s

Holy Fire http://www.holyfire.org/eng

Metropolitan Hilarion https://youtu.be/acVw6N1uM6A

Mikveh https://www.youtube.com/watch?v=ofnBSNGWdfY

Manufactured by Amazon.ca
Bolton, ON

51145463R00094